AMERICAN
WAR LIBRARY

★ ★ ★

★ **World War II** ★

KAMIKAZES

by Earle Rice Jr.

Lucent Books, P.O. Box 289011, San Diego, CA 92198-9011

Titles in The American War Library series include:

World War II
Hitler and the Nazis
Kamikazes
Leaders and Generals
Life as a POW
Life of an American Soldier in
  Europe
Strategic Battles in Europe
Strategic Battles in the Pacific
The War at Home
Weapons of War

The Civil War
Leaders of the North and South
Life Among the Soldiers and
  Cavalry
Lincoln and the Abolition of
  Slavery
Strategic Battles
Weapons of War

Library of Congress Cataloging-in-Publication Data
Rice, Earle, Jr.
    Kamikazes / Earle Rice Jr.
        p.   cm.—(The American war library series)
    Includes bibliographical references and index.
    Summary: Examines the events and personalities that were
instrumental in Japan's adoption of kamikaze, or suicide, missions
in the later stages of World War II.
    ISBN 1-56006-373-4 (lib. : alk. paper)
    1. World War, 1939–1945—Aerial operations, Japanese
Juvenile literature. 2. Japan. Kaigun. Kamikaze Tokubetsu
Kōgekitai—History Juvenile literature. 3. World War, 1939–1945—
Campaigns—Pacific Area Juvenile literature. 4. Suicide—Japan—
Psychological aspects Juvenile literature. [1. World War, 1939–1945
—Aerial operations, Japanese. 2. World War, 1939–1945—
Campaigns—Pacific Ocean. 3. Suicide—Japan—Psychological
aspects.] I. Title. II. Series.
D792.J3R52   2000
940.54'4952—dc21   99-23543
                                                          CIP

Copyright 2000 by Lucent Books, Inc.
P.O. Box 289011, San Diego, California 92198-9011

Printed in the U.S.A.

★ Contents ★

A Nation Forged by War

The United States, like many nations, was forged and defined by war. Despite Benjamin Franklin's opinion that "There never was a good war or a bad peace," the United States owes its very existence to the War of Independence, one to which Franklin wholeheartedly subscribed. The country forged by war in 1776 was tempered and made stronger by the Civil War in the 1860s.

The Texas Revolution, the Mexican-American War, and the Spanish-American War expanded the country's borders and gave it overseas possessions. These wars made the United States a world power, but this status came with a price, as the nation became a key but reluctant player in both World War I and World War II.

Each successive war further defined the country's role on the world stage. Following World War II, U.S. foreign policy redefined itself to focus on the role of defender, not only of the freedom of its own citizens, but also of the freedom of peo-

ple everywhere. During the cold war that followed World War II until the collapse of the Soviet Union, defending the world meant fighting communism. This goal, manifested in the Korean and Vietnam conflicts, proved elusive, and soured the American public on its achievability. As the United States emerged as the world's sole superpower, American foreign policy has been guided less by national interest and more on protecting international human rights. But as involvement in Somalia and Kosovo prove, this goal has been equally elusive.

As a result, the country's view of itself changed. Bolstered by victories in World Wars I and II, Americans first relished the role of protector. But, as war followed war in a seemingly endless procession, Americans began to doubt their leaders, their motives, and themselves. The Vietnam War especially caused people to question the validity of sending its young people to die in places where they were not particularly wanted and for people who did not seem especially grateful.

While the most obvious changes brought about by America's wars have been geopolitical in nature, many other aspects of society have been touched. War often does not bring about change directly, but acts instead like the catalyst in a chemical reaction, accelerating changes already in progress.

Some of these changes have been societal. The role of women in the United States had been slowly changing, but World War II put thousands into the workforce and into uniform. They might have gone back to being housewives after the war, but equality, once experienced, would not be forgotten.

Likewise, wars have accelerated technological change. The necessity for faster airplanes and a more destructive bomb led to the development of jet planes and nuclear energy. Artificial fibers developed for parachutes in the 1940s were used in the clothing of the 1950s.

Lucent Books' American War Library covers key wars in the development of the nation. Each war is covered in several volumes, to allow for more detail, context, and to provide volumes on often neglected subjects, such as the kamikazes of World War II, or weapons used in the Civil War. As with all Lucent Books, notes, annotated bibliographies, and appendixes such as glossaries give students a launching point for further research. In addition, sidebars and archival photographs enhance the text. Together, each volume in The American War Library will aid students in understanding how America's wars have shaped and changed its politics, economics, and society.

One-Way Flights to Eternity

At 0725 on the morning of October 25, 1944, nine Japanese aircraft took to the air out of Mabalacat airfield, on the northernmost Philippine island of Luzon. Their mission: to intercept and destroy American warships that had been reported east of the airfield. They were led by Lieutenant Senior Grade Yukio Seki, command pilot of the *Shikishima* unit—one of the four units of the newly formed *Tokubetsu Kogekitai* (Special Attack Corps or Squad).

Rain squalls and low visibility extended their search and threatened to make them abort their unique mission for a fifth time. But at 1140, Seki radioed his base that he had finally sighted the American warships. They were steaming southward, he reported, about ninety miles east of Tacloban, Leyte.

Despite the murky weather conditions, the *Shikishima* unit had managed to locate the beleaguered Taffy 3 (Task Unit 77.4.3, of the U.S. Seventh Fleet), com-manded by Rear Admiral Clifton A. F. "Ziggy" Sprague.

Zeros Attack Taffy 3

Taffy 3 had started the day with six escort carriers (CVEs), three destroyers (DDs), and four destroyer escorts (DEs). But shortly after 0700, during an impromptu action off Samar, the small task unit had lost an escort carrier, two destroyers, and one destroyer escort to the vastly numerically superior forces of Japanese vice admiral Takeo Kurita. It had also sustained serious damage to two additional CVEs, a DD, and a DE.

The Americans were outgunned but not outfought. At the peak of battle, an officer aboard the CVE *Kitkun Bay* quipped, "It won't be long now, boys; we're sucking 'em into forty millimeter range."[1] His grace under fire belied the inevitable outcome of a match between his 40-millimeter guns and the 18.1-inch guns of Kurita's battleships—peashooters against cannons. Despite the

Military Twenty-Four-Hour Clock

Military times are used throughout the book. This key, showing familiar A.M. and P.M. times paired with the corresponding time on the twenty-four-hour clock, may be helpful in learning the system.

A.M.	24	P.M.	24
1	0100	1	1300
2	0200	2	1400
3	0300	3	1500
4	0400	4	1600
5	0500	5	1700
6	0600	6	1800
7	0700	7	1900
8	0800	8	2000
9	0900	9	2100
10	1000	10	2200
11	1100	11	2300
12	1200	12	2400

American officer's bravado, only Kurita's inexplicable decision to break off the engagement on the verge of total victory ultimately spared Taffy 3 from complete annihilation.

At 0911, the Japanese warships—four battleships, eight cruisers, and eleven destroyers—abruptly turned about and headed north. Their surprise withdrawal dramatically terminated the sea action that future history books would record as the surface phase of the Battle of Samar.

Thankful American sailors stared in near disbelief as Kurita's armada steamed away from Sprague's embattled Taffy 3. A young signalman aboard Admiral Sprague's flagship, the CVE *Fanshaw Bay,* commented, "Damn it, boys, they're getting away!"[2]

About an hour and a half later, the sea appeared deceptively calm and the horizon void of imminent danger. Captain F. J. McKenna, skipper of the escort carrier *St. Lo,* figured that his men, who had stood on full alert since sunrise, needed a break. Accordingly, he secured his crew from general quarters, the state of maximum readiness aboard a warship. Unknown to McKenna, the tranquil skies of the then-calm battle zone were about to explode in a thunderous roar of unprecedented aerial action.

The nine Japanese Zeros of the *Shikishima* unit—five laden with 550-pound bombs and four flying fighter escort— were at that moment closing fast on Taffy 3's five remaining CVEs and their four smaller escorts. The planes were skimming the wave tops to avoid detection by radar or by Combat Air Patrols (CAPs) flying thousands of feet overhead. Minutes before reaching the ships of Taffy 3, the Zeros pulled up sharply to five thousand feet and dove into the attack.

At 1053, Lieutenant Seki plunged his bomb-laden plane into the *St. Lo*. A second pilot followed Seki down and rammed his plane into the hapless CVE in almost the exact same spot. Fearful explosions ripped the small carrier apart. Captain McKenna ordered his crew to abandon ship. The *St. Lo* disappeared beneath the sea at 1125.

Meanwhile, a third bomb-laden Zero crashed into the CVE *Kalinin Bay*, exploding against her flight deck and inflicting awesome damage. At about the same time,

A fireball erupts from the flight deck of the St. Lo *as a result of two kamikaze strikes. The carrier did not survive the ordeal.*

the fourth and fifth bomb-carrying Zeros targeted two different CVEs. One smashed into the *Kitkun Bay;* the other slammed into the *White Plains.* Wracked by explosions and seared by fire, the two carriers shuddered and smoked but refused to sink.

A New, Horrifying Weapon

At 1130 the four escort Zeros turned toward home to report a successful mission. Admiral Sprague then ordered the all clear sounded. Eight of his original thirteen ships had survived the day—but just barely. Radio Tokyo wasted no time in broadcasting the news of a great Japanese victory:

> The *Shikishima* unit of the Kamikaze Special Attack Corps made a successful surprise attack on an enemy task force containing four [*sic*] aircraft carriers at a point thirty miles northeast Suluan Island at ten forty-five. Two planes hit one carrier, which was definitely sunk. A third plane hit another carrier, setting it aflame. A fourth hit a cruiser, which sank instantly [*sic*].[3]

This report clearly left Japanese ship recognition and battle reporting open to question: No cruisers formed a part of Taffy 3; neither was any ship other than the *St. Lo* sunk by the suicidal attacks of

Rear Admiral Clifton Sprague aboard the flagship of the Taffy 3 task unit. Calm moments such as this would soon be shattered by the kamikazes.

Lieutenant Seki and his comrades. More important, however, the success of their mission lent credence to a new, horrifying weapon that would strike terror into the hearts of Japan's enemies—primarily American sailors—for the remaining ten months of World War II.

Thus, on October 25, 1944, the last day of the Battle of Leyte Gulf—the greatest naval engagement in all of history—a new word was added to the vernacular of modern warfare: *kamikaze!*

The Divine Wind

Born of desperation and bred on the lifeblood of mostly fledgling pilots, the Kamikaze Special Attack Corps was organized by Japan's high command late in the war. Japanese strategists hoped to turn back the enemy advance using suicidal attacks by volunteer pilots assigned to crash their bomb-laden aircraft into Allied warships. It seemed to many of Japan's top military leaders that an exchange of one Japanese pilot and plane for one enemy warship represented a worthwhile return on their investment. (It is worth mentioning that command officials with the authority to sanction such suicide flights generally did not themselves have to fly them.)

One pilot, one ship. Struck by antiaircraft fire, a suicide pilot continues his one-way attack against an American escort carrier.

The first official sanction for the use of suicide as a weapon came at a special conference requested by Emperor Hirohito and held at the Imperial Palace in Tokyo on June 25, 1944. Top army and navy leaders apprised the emperor of the deepening crisis facing Japan. After the emperor had retired to his chambers, Prince Hiroyasu Fushimi—the grizzled, sixty-nine-year-old senior fleet admiral of the Imperial Japanese Navy (IJN)—addressed the gathering and, in part, said:

> In present-day wars, both friend and enemy use almost identical weapons and other essentials of war. In matters such as radar, our enemy is superior to us qualitatively and quantitatively. Results favorable to us cannot be expected unless improvements are effected in these matters. Both the Army and the Navy must think up some special [that is, suicide] weapons and conduct the war with them. This is urgent. Now that the war situation has reached this difficult stage, special [suicide] aircraft, warships, and small vessels need to be deployed and quickly used.[4]

The following day, Emperor Hirohito summoned the army and navy chiefs of staff, General Hideki Tojo and Admiral Shigetaro Shimada, respectively, to inform them that he approved of greater cooperation between the air arms of the army and navy through a committee established to accelerate the preparation of "special attack weapons."[5]

Achieving anything more than token cooperation between two services that were traditionally at cross-purposes was supremely optimistic on the emperor's part. But both the army and navy had already embarked on numerous developmental programs for "special attack" (or suicide) weapons by then. The Kamikaze Special Attack Corps was destined to become not only the most famous of Japan's suicide weapons but also the most effective.

The inspiration and motivation for this unique corps of pilots dedicated to self-destruction in the name of emperor and country were rooted in Japanese religious and cultural traditions, and in the way of the samurai (members of the warrior aristocracy of medieval Japan). Even the name *kamikaze*, which means "divine wind" in Japanese, resonates with religious overtones that harken back to the thirteenth century.

A kamikaze unit poses for what may be their last photograph. Pilots of the "divine wind" died with the hope that their self-sacrifice would turn the tide of the war.

In 1274, and again in 1281, Kublai Khan, the Mongol ruler of China, assembled great fleets and attempted to invade the Japanese island of Kyushu. On both occasions, according to legend, prayers to the Japanese wind god Ise were answered: At the crucial point in both invasion attempts, a storm of extraordinary fury—the Divine Wind or Typhoon—suddenly arose, battering the Mongol fleet and forcing its withdrawal.

Although the role of the samurai in repelling the invaders often receives little or no coverage in history books, their part, irrespective of Ise's "divine" intervention, cannot be overstated. Stephen Turnbull, a military historian noted for his work on the Japanese samurai, notes:

> Decisive though the typhoon was [in both instances], it would have been minimal in its effectiveness if the determination and fighting qualities of the samurai had not forced the entire fleet to lie at anchor with all their armies aboard, cooped up by the ferocity of Japanese raids in little ships, and unable to establish a beachhead because of the tenacity with which the land was defended.[6]

Plainly, the Japanese owed their thirteenth-century deliverance from the Mongols not only to a god-induced miracle but rather more to the fighting prowess of the samurai. In sum, it is probably fair to say that

Mongol ships are pictured here on their way to invade Japan in 1281. The fleet was turned back by a typhoon known thereafter by the Japanese as the kamikaze, *or "divine wind."*

either force acting alone could not have repulsed the Mongol invaders.

Walking Dead Men

The term *kamikaze* took on new meaning in 1944, when Japan's war leaders likened the American threat to their home islands to the unsuccessful Mongol invasion attempts of more than six and a half centuries earlier. This comparative link to past heroics inspired a new generation of samurai to resist—to a certain death—a latter-day attack on their homeland. Writes Turnbull:

> It has in it all the finest elements of Japanese tradition. There are noble samurai, united against a common enemy, and fired by a common spirit which later manifests itself in the cataclysm of the holy typhoon. For once in

their history the samurai are not fighting each other, but become Japanese before anything else.[7]

The annals of history bulge with accounts of warriors laying down their lives in defense of their country. The willingness of soldiers to sacrifice their lives for cause and country in time of war is as old as war itself and forms an intrinsic and vital part of all successful military organizations.

Japanese foot soldiers on Guadalcanal in 1942 were among the first to exhibit the self-sacrificing spirit of their people, choosing to die in suicidal attacks known as banzai charges rather than surrender. ("Banzai!" in the context of a battle cry, meant roughly, "Hail to the Emperor! May he live for ten thousand years!") Fewer than one in twenty Japanese soldiers surrendered on Guadalcanal during any one battle—and most of those taken prisoner were either badly wounded or unconscious. Not surprisingly, one Guadalcanal veteran observed, "The Japanese seem to get a grotesque pleasure from self-destruction . . . whether by their own hand or by the hand of others."[8]

From the start of the Pacific War until late 1944, many incidents were recorded of Japanese pilots deliberately crashing their planes into American warships. Most of these acts resulted from the individual initiative of badly wounded pilots or of pilots in severely damaged aircraft, which in either case deprived the pilot of any reasonable chance of returning safely to base. Nor

Two Heroes

History records many individual acts of heroic self-sacrifice in the Pacific Theater during World War II. In *I Was a Kamikaze*, Ryuji Nagatsuka writes of two Japanese heroes whose acts played a significant role in the development of the kamikaze concept:

> The history of suicide-attacks dates from October, 1944. It was [Major Katsushige] Takada [Takata], commandant of the 5th Army Squadron [Flying Regiment], who first attempted this kind of attack. He had deliberately crashed his plane on an enemy ship during the Battle of Biak Island [off the coast of West New Guinea], at the end of May, 1944. And in mid-October, Rear Admiral [Masabumi] Arima's plane, damaged by bullets, had dived down in an effort to strike an American carrier during the Battle of Formosa. It fell into the sea close by without reaching the ship. However, the suicide-attacks carried out by these two heroes were not preconceived and planned. It was October 20 that the first collective special attack squad was officially formed under the leadership of naval Lieutenant Yukio Seki.

were such incidents of self-sacrifice limited to the Japanese.

Early in the war at Midway, for example, marine pilot Captain Richard E. Fleming, either by design or accident, crashed his flaming Vindicator dive-bomber into the Japanese heavy cruiser *Mikuma*'s aft turret. Japanese air group commander Mitsuo Fuchida, who witnessed Fleming's final act, called it an attempt at "a daring suicide crash."[9] Flames from the fiery wreck of Fleming's bomber were sucked into the air intake of the cruiser's starboard engine room, igniting gas fumes and killing everyone inside.

Traditionally, then, warriors have voluntarily laid down their lives in battle for the greater good. There is nothing new in that premise. What was new about the kamikaze concept was that the sacrifice of one's life was not only *expected*, it was *scheduled in advance*. "Military history teems with situations in which there was only a 10 per cent chance of survival," wrote Flight Lieutenant Ryuji Nagatsuka, a former kamikaze pilot who survived the war, "but one that left no possible chance at all was unique."[10] And

The wreckage of marine pilot Captain Richard E. Fleming's Vindicator dive-bomber can be seen here on the aft turret of the sinking Japanese cruiser Mikuma.

once bound to this unique concept of programmed self-sacrifice, kamikaze pilots became walking dead men—with no possibility of reprieve.

The Kamikaze Mystique

Many Western observers of the kamikaze mystique, particularly those unfamiliar with Eastern thinking, find it hard to accept the moral legitimacy of a program based on mass self-destruction. Suicide violates the basic teachings of Western law and religion and is accordingly dishonored and condemned. The Japanese moral code, on the other hand, has long esteemed self-extinction as both honorable and preferable to living in shame.

A brief review of Japanese attitudes toward voluntary death and the sources of their suicidal thinking might help to explain why thousands of young Japanese pilots like Ryuji Nagatsuka willingly—often even *eagerly*—volunteered to fly one-way flights to eternity.

Chapter 1

Japan and the Sources of Suicide

"The soldier and sailor should consider loyalty their essential duty. . . . With [a] single heart fulfill your essential duty of loyalty, and bear in mind that duty is weightier than a mountain, while death is lighter than a feather."

—from the "Imperial Rescript to Soldiers and Sailors," issued by Emperor Meiji in 1882 (quoted in Yasuo Kuwahara and Gordon T. Allred, *Kamikaze*)

During World War II, the willingness of both Japan's military ranks and civilian populaces to choose the finality of suicide over the shame attached to surrender derives from a variety of religious, cultural, political, and philosophical convictions embodied in the Japanese heritage. Eastern religions, belief in a divine origin (emperor worship) and a predestiny to rule the world (the *hakko ichiu* principle), the Bushido code, *gyokusai* (glorious self-annihilation), and the resultant morality and its effect on an evolving military machine—all these factors and more contributed to the kamikaze phenomenon.

Boye De Mente, author of more than twenty books on Asian cultures, writes:

Fighting to the death regardless of the odds and chances of success was a deeply embedded tradition in Japan. In fact, the greater the likelihood of defeat, the more certain it was that the Japanese would fight to the death in battle or kill themselves following defeat. To begin to understand the mentality that led Japan to make suicide attacks an official part of its war effort, one must know a great deal about her past.[11]

Although the origins of the Japanese people are uncertain, most students of their history believe that they are of mixed ancestry, with a dominant strain of immigrants from the northern Asian mainland, coupled with a lesser strain from the south-eastern coastal areas of Asia. Some anthropologists also support the lesser likelihood of Indonesian or Polynesian strains. In any case, the origins of the deeply mystical Japanese intellect that so readily embraced the spirit of self-sacrifice can be said to have derived in no small measure from Amaterasu-o-Mikami, the Sun Goddess, sometimes called the Great Ancestress of the Japanese.

Shinto and the Emperor Ideology

Legend holds that the Japanese islands were created by the god Izanagi (The Male Who Invites) and the goddess Izanami (The Female Who Invites). It is written that this divine couple stood on the floating Bridge of Heaven and dipped a spear into the ocean below. Droplets of water from the spear's point then condensed in the ocean to form the sacred islands of Japan.

Harry Cook, an author and journalist who specializes in Oriental history, writes:

> To populate these islands, the gods created a large number of divine and semi-divine beings, one of whom claimed direct descent from the Sun Goddess, Amaterasu, and as such held a divine mandate to rule. The mountains, rivers, lakes, trees, and other natural manifestations were also divine and regarded as kami, or spirits.[12]

Shinto (The Way of the Gods), Japan's native religion, is rooted chiefly in the cultic devotion to these *kami* (deities of natu-

From Heaven, the god Izanagi and the goddess Izanami dip a spear into the ocean. Legend held that the droplets from the spear created the islands of Japan.

ral forces) and to the veneration of the emperor as a direct descendant of the Sun Goddess.

One version of the Japanese foundation myth credits Izanami with giving birth to Amaterasu, while another account claims that Amaterasu emerged from the left eye of Izanagi (and the Moon God from his right eye) during a purification rite. Irrespective of her vague beginnings, Amaterasu is said to have formed a liaison with a Korean trader-pirate at about the time of Christ. As a result of their union, the Korean plunderer became the great grandfather of Japan's first emperor, Jimmu Tenno (reigned 660–585 B.C.), and the direct ancestor of Japan's 124th emperor, Hirohito (reigned 1926–1989), in an unbroken link. (Jimmu ascended the Japanese throne in 660 B.C., a date that is still officially celebrated as the foundation of the Japanese state.)

Unlike the religions of Buddha and Christ that were brought to Japan, Shinto is native to Japan and dates back to the nation's beginnings. In simple terms, it is a loose system of beliefs and attitudes held by most Japanese about themselves, one another, and the ruling powers. Followers of Shinto revere the *kami*, which can be neither known nor explained by mortals, as the source of human life and existence. Through their superior powers, either natural or divine, the *kami* reveal truth to the people and guide them on their path.

Shinto does not conduct regular weekly services, but devotees may visit any of its many shrines at any time.

Shintoism is closely aligned with the nation's system of values and the behavior of its people. From the late 1800s until the close of World War II in 1945, the Japanese government supported a state Shinto and used

It was believed that the first emperor of Japan, Jimmu Tenno (top), was born of a divine mother. Emperor Hirohito (below) was a direct descendant of this half-divine line.

it to promote nationalism, excite patriotic zeal, and facilitate military preparations for war. The emperor, as head of the Shinto religion, played a vital role in all three categories. He stood for paternal love, family values, and national harmony, but his rule was oppressive. Of the emperor ideology incorporated into Shinto, Yuri Tanaka, a Japanese historian of today's generation, comments:

> The emperor ideology had a tendency toward totalitarianism from the beginning, but this tendency was veiled with mysticism, and as a result the illusory concept of the harmony of the nation was established. The two concepts of familial love among all Japanese people and harmony within the nation served to disguise the oppression of the Japanese by their rulers. Thus, in the minds of many, the emperor became the key figure in maintaining national harmony. It seemed natural to demonstrate strong loyalty to him in return for the "social welfare" he provided.[13]

As Tanaka points out, the modern Japanese state, predicated on the emperor system, did not take root overnight. The concept of a family-state originated in the late nineteenth century and reached the point of full development about 1910. Left-wing politics then flourished in Japan for about ten years. But a movement toward fascism, which embraced the notion of family-state, emerged in the 1920s and became solidly entrenched during

In present-day Tokyo, Shinto priests are seen here on their way to perform a traditional rite. The emperor of Japan was once the head of this religion.

The Sacred Throne

In February 1941, while addressing three thousand primary school teachers at Hibuya Hall in Tokyo, Prime Minister Kiichiro Hiranuma commemorated the "2601st Anniversary of the Founding of the Japanese Empire." In *Kamikaze: Japan's Suicide Samurai*, Japanologist and historian Raymond Lamont-Brown recalls a portion of Hiranuma's speech, which lauds Japan's divine origins:

> Japan's national polity [government or state] is unique in the world. Heaven sent down Niningi-no-Mikoto [grandson of Sun Goddess Amaterasu-o-Mikami] to Kishihara in Yamato Province with a message that their posterity should reign over and govern Japan for ages eternal. It was on this day, 2601 years ago, that our first Emperor, Jimmu, ascended the Throne. Dynasties in foreign countries were created by men. Foreign kings, emperors and presidents are all created by men, but Japan has a Sacred Throne inherited from the Imperial Ancestors; Japanese Imperial Rule, therefore, is an extension of Heaven. Dynasties created by men may collapse, but the Heaven-created Throne is beyond men's power.

the first half of the 1930s. The high point of the movement came in the period between 1936 and August 1945 following the entrenchment of fascism. "In short," concludes Yuri Tanaka, "the emperor ideology, based upon the family-state concept, gradually penetrated the Japanese mind from around 1910, became strongly entrenched during the 1920s, then fed into Japanese fascism from the 1930s." [14]

The emperor ideology—that is, emperor worship and blind obedience to him—possibly contributed more than any other single factor to the deaths of nearly 1.75 million Japanese combatants in World War II. With regard to the kamikazes, at least, Emperor Hirohito's approval of Japan's special attack strategies has to rank with history's most outrageous betrayals and abuses of power.

Of Ancestors and Afterlife

In addition to their native Shinto—a religion without formulated, readily expressed tenets or sacred books comparable to the Bible or the Koran—the Japanese were also strongly influenced by the Chinese doctrine of Confucianism and more strongly yet by the Chinese interpretation of Buddhism. (Christianity—introduced into Japan in the sixteenth century by the Spanish Jesuit Francis Xavier— had a far lesser impact on the Japanese. Even today, for example, there are fewer than one million Christians in Japan.)

Confucianism, although generally considered a religion, is more accurately defined as a system of moral conduct. Founded in China some twenty-five hundred years ago by Confucius (551–479 B.C.), its ideals and humane philosophy have since influenced all of eastern Asia. Confucius, rather than teaching about any god, focused his efforts on making people better in their lifetime. Filial love, fraternal duty, and respect for ancestors represent several aspects of Confucianism that hold particular relevance for the Japanese. With regard to ancestor veneration, James R. Ware, an expert on Chinese culture, writes, "It [the doctrine of Confucianism] teaches man to see himself correctly as the descendant of a long ancestry to which he owes respect and gratitude for his temporary gift of personal existence."[15]

Faced with surrender or death during World War II, most Japanese combatants opted to die rather than dishonor their family or their ancestors. Even during the final days of the war, when all hope of a Japanese victory had faded, kamikaze pilots still flew to their deaths, many for no other reason than to avoid bringing shame upon their loved ones. No doubt the Buddhist teachings that "life goes on and on in many reincarnations or rebirths"[16] brought solace to many pilots on their final flight.

Buddhism—a complex system of beliefs based on the teachings of the Buddha, Siddhārtha Gautama (563–483 B.C.)—originated in India about twenty-five hundred years ago. Various forms of the religion spread across eastern Asia over the ensuing centuries. One Chinese sect of Buddhism called Ch'an ("Zen" in Japanese) gained dominance in Korea about the fifth century.

Good fortunes and paper money are burned during a rite honoring those who have passed into the afterlife. Confucius taught that the living owe respect and gratitude to their ancestors.

From there it was brought to Japan by Korean missionaries, between 550 and 600, where it flourished and still flourishes.

Buddhism added texture and dimension to Japanese religious thought. "Almost every Japanese household [during World War II] had two shrines—one Buddhist, one Shinto," writes John Toland, a popular American historian who has written extensively about Japan and the Pacific War. Particularly appealing to the Japanese were the Buddhist teachings of journeying through the pain of the present world to the bliss of the next and Buddhism's impassive attitude toward death. Toland observes:

> This strong recognition of death gave the Japanese not only the strength to face disaster stoically but an intense appreciation of each moment, which could be the last. This was not pessimism but a calm determination to let nothing discourage or disappoint or elate, to accept the inevitable.[17]

An image of the Buddha. Along with Shinto and Confucianism, Buddhism formed the heart of Japanese spirituality.

Clearly, then, the Eastern religions that together made up the core of Japanese spirituality—principally Shinto, Confucianism, and Buddhism—constituted a chief component of the Japanese psyche, which accepted suicide or self-sacrifice not only as a moral act but as a legitimate means to an end. A second key contributor in modeling the Japanese spirit of self-sacrifice can be found in the Bushido code.

The Bushido Code

During the Japanese feudal age (1185–1600), the authority of the emperors was diminished to only token status by state-appointed military governors called *shugo*, under a shogun, or chief military commander. But even the shogun's power was usurped by local lords known as *daimyo*, who divided the country into feudal domains. For several centuries, warrior leaders fought one another for land and vassals (subordinates). Commencing in the eleventh century, the samurai or *bushi* (Japanese terms used interchangeably for "warrior" or "warriors") began to earn prominence as protectors of either the *daimyo* domains or the shogun provinces.

Samurai—the Eastern counterparts to the knights of medieval Europe—lived by a strict code of conduct called Bushido (*bushi*, "warrior" + *do*, "way"—The Way of the Warrior) that emerged in about the thirteenth century. The samurai's chief virtue, as defined by his creed, was the ability to decide on a proper course of action and pursue that course without wavering—in short, to

strike at the right time and to die at the right moment. Countless kamikazes took this samurai virtue to heart and made it their own during World War II.

But the virtue of unwavering decisiveness forms only a part of the warrior's creed. Like the European knight's code of chivalry, the samurai's code of conduct, or Bushido, was a complex set of values and

Heavily armed Samurai warriors of thirteenth-century Japan patrol the streets of a small town. Samurai virtue lived on in many of the kamikazes.

rules for governing his behavior. Scholarly attempts to define the cardinal principles of Bushido vary in both quantity and interpretation. Japanese historian Yuri Tanaka, in a fairly typical representation of Bushido's details, identifies its "seven essential elements" as paraphrased here:

1. Righteousness: commitment to justice and duty and despising of cowardice;

2. Courage: the will to do right and an indomitable spirit in the face of adversity, including death; to die for a just cause is the highest honor;

3. Humanity: a particular requirement for leaders; humanity toward the weak or the defeated is seen as a most honorable way for a warrior to conduct himself;

4. Propriety: the realization of humanity in acts of kindness;

5. Sincerity: the respect for truth and the avoidance of lying;

6. Honor: the realization of one's own duty and privilege; the honorable warrior can do no wrong without feeling great shame;

7. Loyalty: obedience to one's seniors but never blind obedience.

"In summary," Tanaka concludes, "it can be seen from the elements of the code that *bushido* requires great self-discipline together with great tolerance toward others."[18]

As Japan emerged from its feudal age and moved through a period of national unification under the Tokugawa shogunate (1600–1853), respect for Bushido tenets transcended the warrior class. "The tradi-tions and values that had been special to the samurai class were highly respected by many Japanese," writes Harry Cook, "and Bushido—the warrior's code—became an expression of national morality."[19]

Although the need for samurai ended in 1868 with the Meiji Restoration (which restored the emperor's authority and marked Japan's entrance into the modern age), esteem for the tenets of Bushido carried over into modernity—albeit with changes. As the emperor ideology was evolving and becoming established in Japanese society, military ethics and philosophies were undergoing related changes aimed at subordinating Bushido to the emperor ideology and the new military doctrine. By 1920 the true spirit of Bushido had all but disappeared from Japan's armed forces, and what remained of it was little more than a hollow echo of a once-vibrant creed.

Glorious Death and World Domination

Over the next twenty years, Japanese militarists continued to subvert their new code of military conduct, intent on instilling a sense of *gyokusai*—glorious self-annihilation—among the officers and the rank and file of Japan's armed forces. The word *gyokusai* (literally, "broken gem") comes from the Chinese *Book of North Chi*, a chronicle of the brief Chi dynasty (A.D. 550–577). The book includes this statement: "Men of strength [heroes] prefer to become gems to break into myriad fragments than to become roof tiles to live out their lives in idleness."[20] Death, cried Japan's military chiefs, was always to be preferred over surrender. Blind obedience became a way of life in the Japanese armed services.

On January 3, 1941, less than a year before the Japanese attack on Pearl Harbor, General Hideki Tojo (then army minister) issued a new official code of ethics to every member of the armed forces. Entitled *Senjin Kun* (*Ethics of Battle*), it included this admonishment:

> Do not think of death as you use up every ounce of your strength to fulfill your duties. Make it your joy to use every last bit of your physical and spiritual strength in what you do. Do not fear to die for the cause of everlasting justice. Do not stay alive in dishonor. Do not die in such a way as to leave a bad name behind you.[21]

Among other things, Tojo's new military code called for soldiers to commit suicide rather than surrender. (Ritual suicide or *seppuku*—disembowelment known in the more vulgar vernacular as *hara-kiri*—had been considered an honorable death since the time of the samurai.) Moreover, *Gunjin Chokuron* (*Imperial Code of Military Conduct*) required absolute loyalty to the emperor. Every soldier who died for

General Hideki Tojo's military philosophies greatly influenced the kamikaze pilots. He exhorted all soldiers to die in honor rather than surrender in shame.

Part of the Japanese warrior tradition of an honorable death included seppuku, *in which a soldier ritually disemboweled himself rather than be killed by the enemy.*

the emperor expected his own spirit to reside at Tokyo's *Yasukuni-jinja* (war memorial) on Kudan Hill, among the spirits of all of Japan's war dead.

At Yasukuni Shrine (Shrine of the Righteous Souls), their souls gained a kind of immortality. "The dead did not die but waited, enshrined and deified, until called to fight alongside the living," write historians Denis and Peggy Warner and Sadao Seno. "The spirit of Yasukuni and of *Yamato* (Great Peace), the old name for Japan, was instilled into all men of the Japanese forces."[22]

The Japanese soldier believed that his life would continue through the spirit of the emperor, or *kokutai* (the national body). Untold numbers of kamikazes bade farewell to their comrades with such adieus as "I'll be waiting for you at Yasukuni Shrine"[23] or "See you at Yasukuni Temple!"[24] Their spirits and sacrifices are still honored by thousands of annual visitors to the shrine.

During the first four decades of the twentieth century, then, the idea of glorious self-sacrifice (*gyokusai*) in the name of the emperor and for the good of the nation took root in the Japanese spirit, or *Yamato-damashii*. What's more, as Japan's militarists edged Japan closer to war with

Not What They Seemed

Students of Japan's role in World War II often disagree as to what motivated kamikaze pilots to fly their one-way death missions. In *Eagle Against the Sun: The American War with Japan,* military historian Ronald H. Spector suggests that their motivations were not what they seemed:

> To the American sailors and airmen who were on the receiving end of these relentless tactics of self-destruction, the kamikazes seemed motivated by a kind of supreme fanaticism. They appeared to be a sort of super-samurai who believed that in dying for the Emperor, they would achieve immortality in some heroes' paradise. In fact, most kamikaze pilots were not professional warriors but recent university students or graduates who were not particularly religious and had no expectation of a blissful or heroic afterlife. They were motivated by the traditional Japanese feeling of *"on,"* or obligation

and gratitude toward their family or country, and by the traditional Japanese admiration for noble death in a worthy if hopeless cause.

Most kamikaze pilots were not motivated by religious fanaticism, but rather by a personal sense of obligation to their families and country.

Japanese servicemen are seen marching through Tokyo in 1934 to pay tribute to all of Japan's fallen war heroes at Yasukuni Shrine.

mission—destined to rule first Asia and then the world.

This bit of propagandizing formed the basis for the *hakko ichiu* principle—"the whole world under one roof,"[25] which really meant under the emperor. So, armed with an unswerving devotion to their emperor and an unshakable faith in their ordained destiny, the Japanese people embarked on their "spiritual mission" of world domination. Their venture resulted in what amounted to *seppuku* at the national level.

the United States, they capitalized on the belief of the Japanese people in their divine origin, convincing them that they were chosen people on a great spiritual

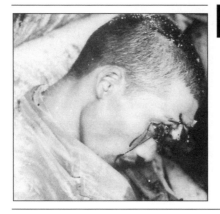

Chapter 2

"A Fitting Place to Die"

"Inferiors should regard the orders of their superiors as issuing directly from the Emperor. . . . Except when official duty requires them to be strict and severe, superiors should treat their inferiors with consideration, making kindness their chief aim, so that all grades may unite in their service to the Emperor."

—from the "Imperial Rescript to Soldiers and Sailors"

Japanese efforts to implement the *hakko ichiu* principle advanced with lightning speed for the first six months of Japan's war with the United States and its allies. But the tide of war started to turn with a striking American naval victory at Midway in June 1942. With the subsequent American invasion of Japanese-held Guadalcanal (in the Solomon Islands) in August 1942, U.S. forces seized the initiative for the first time in the western Pacific Theater and never looked back.

"Hell Is on Us"

Guadalcanal fell to U.S. forces early in 1943, and the primarily American juggernaut con-tinued to advance, rolling back the Japanese defensive perimeter all across the Pacific. As 1944 opened, the sun began to set on Japan's receding empire. America's industrial might and expanding resources in men, machines, and technological advances had taken a heavy toll on the Japanese in 1943.

During an intense campaign against Japan's merchant marine, American submarines sank close to 300 Japanese merchantmen and sent some 1.3 million valuable tons of enemy shipping to the bottom of the sea. These losses represented about 700,000 tons more than the Japanese were able to replace within the same time frame.

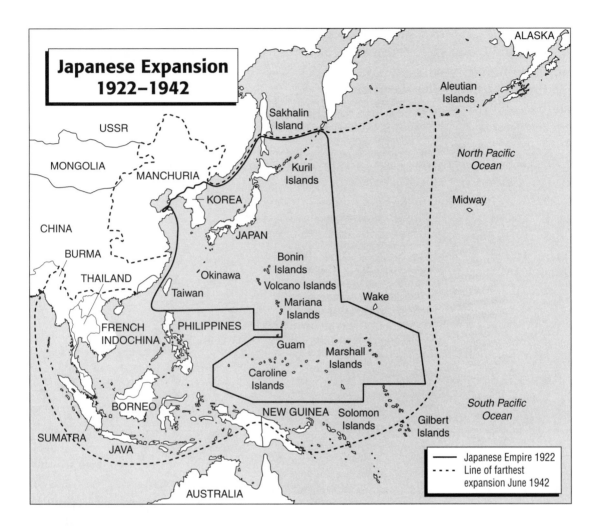

Japanese Expansion 1922–1942

ALASKA

Aleutian Islands

USSR

North Pacific Ocean

MONGOLIA

Sakhalin Island

Midway

MANCHURIA

Kuril Islands

KOREA

CHINA

JAPAN

BURMA

Okinawa

Bonin Islands

Volcano Islands

THAILAND

Taiwan

Mariana Islands

Wake

FRENCH INDOCHINA

PHILIPPINES

Guam

Marshall Islands

Caroline Islands

BORNEO

NEW GUINEA

Solomon Islands

South Pacific Ocean

Gilbert Islands

SUMATRA

JAVA

AUSTRALIA

—— Japanese Empire 1922
- - - Line of farthest expansion June 1942

Japan, an island nation whose survival depended almost entirely on imports, was being systematically deprived of vital goods and materials but was helpless to prevent the losses. Japan's merchant ships still outnumbered those of the United States, but the Americans accelerated their undersea campaign against Japanese tankers in 1944, and the gap in merchant vessels closed rapidly. "The U.S. submarine offensive against Japan was one of the decisive elements in ensuring Japan's defeat," military historian Ronald H. Spector wrote later. "A force comprising less than 2 percent of U.S. Navy personnel had accounted for 55 percent of Japan's losses at sea." [26]

Worse yet, from a Japanese perspective, the two-branched, island-hopping American counteroffensive in the Pacific gathered great momentum in 1944. Beginning in January, U.S. forces under General Douglas MacArthur racked up a string of victories in the Admiralties and other nearby island groups. At the same time, additional troops under MacArthur pressed steadily forward along the 1,500- mile northern coast of New Guinea and on to the Molucca Islands, culminating their advances in the capture of Morotai on September 15.

Coincidental with MacArthur's telling strikes, the other American spearhead

Marines make their advance on Guadalcanal in early 1943 (above). The American counteroffensive was fortified by submarine strikes (right) against Japanese supply ships.

Admiral Chester W. Nimitz (left) assembled a naval force of over five hundred ships under the command of Admiral Raymond A. Spruance (right) for the assault against Saipan.

mada of more than five hundred ships under the command of Admiral Raymond A. Spruance—a hero of America's first naval victory against Japan at Midway. On June 15, Spruance launched an amphibious assault against Saipan, in the Marianas, in the face of fierce Japanese resistance.

To help repulse the American invasion force, the Japanese sent a fleet from the Philippines of 9 carriers, 18 battleships and cruisers, and 28 destroyers. Vice Admiral Marc A. Mitscher's U.S. force of 15 carriers, 7 battleships, 21 cruisers, and 69 destroyers clashed with the Japanese fleet in the vicinity of Guam during June 19–21. This engagement, in which Mitscher's Task Force 58 (TF 58) struck a mortal blow to Japanese airpower, is officially designated the Battle of the Philippine Sea. But American pilots, who bagged ten planes for every one lost, unofficially dubbed the three-day shoot-out the Great Marianas Turkey Shoot. The final count totaled 300 Japanese planes lost against 29 American losses. Commented Admiral Mitscher, "Jap planes still burn very well."[27]

But following the Turkey Shoot and the fighting for Saipan, not many Japanese planes remained to be burned, observed

under Admiral Chester W. Nimitz was enjoying similar successes in the Solomon and Marshall Islands and on Eniwetok atoll. In late spring, Nimitz amassed an ar-

future kamikaze Ryuji Nagatsuka, then in training at Utsunomiya airfield on Japan's main island of Honshu. "After Saipan, our navy had only four aircraft carriers left, and there were not more than 2,500 aircraft in all," he writes. "It was obvious that Japan had no hope at all of regaining supremacy on the sea or in the air."[28]

After the fall of Saipan on July 9, Japanese prime minister General Hideki Tojo declared, "Japan is threatened by a national crisis without precedent."[29] Tojo, who had earlier scoffed at the possibility of an American invasion of the Marianas, resigned his office under pressure nine days later.

The following month, Nimitz's naval and amphibious forces completed their conquest of the Marianas, capturing Tinian on August 2 and Guam eight days later. They then continued westward to strike Peleliu in the Palau Islands (part of the western Carolines) on September 15. With Nimitz's forces holding Peleliu and MacArthur's ensconced on Morotai, the

Pilots aboard the Lexington *celebrate their victories over the Japanese in the Great Marianas Turkey Shoot.*

"A Dreadful Commonplace"

As U.S. forces advanced closer to Japan in their island-hopping campaign in the Pacific, the stiffening Japanese resistance amazed the American troops. In *Thunder Gods: The Kamikaze Pilots Tell Their Story,* Hatsuho Naito—a Japanese historian and former naval officer during World War II—explains why:

> All during Japan's long feudal age (which actually did not end until 1945), to fail in battle or to be captured was not acceptable. . . .

> As the situation worsened for Japanese troops on the various islands of the Pacific, both servicemen and civilians were ordered to fight to the death, and to kill themselves if they were wounded and unable to fight. The *banzai* (literally "10,000 years"—a word expressing group resolution) charge by outnumbered and outfought Japanese troops became a

dreadful commonplace. Mass suicides astounded the Americans. They did not know what to think of such an enemy. Nothing in their history, nothing in their experience, had prepared them to understand such behavior.

These Japanese marines committed suicide in their bunker rather than face capture by American troops. The soldier in the rear used his toe to pull the trigger of his rifle.

Americans halted their island-hopping advance momentarily to reassess their strategy and coordinate their next move.

On Morotai, General MacArthur and an aide proceeded to a point on the island nearest the Philippines and gazed toward the northwest. In a barely audible voice, MacArthur said, "They are waiting for me there. They have been waiting a long time."[30]

Meanwhile, in Japan, an unnamed official commented, "Hell is on us."[31] Few of his colleagues disagreed.

A Japanese Plan for Decisive Action

American strategy for Japan's defeat had been settled in principle at a conference at Pearl Harbor in July 1944, attended by MacArthur, Nimitz, and President Franklin D. Roosevelt. Final approval of where to strike next did not come until mid-October, however, at an Anglo-American conference in Quebec, code-named OCTAGON. Attending were Roosevelt, British prime minister Winston Churchill, and their respective military and diplomatic advisers. The

A Massive Suicide Attack

Japanese soldiers demonstrated their suicidal tendencies again and again during the Pacific War. In *Warriors of the Rising Sun: A History of the Japanese Military*, UCLA professor and historian Robert B. Edgerton recounts their savage banzai attacks on Saipan:

> In June 1944, about 20,000 marines came ashore without opposition but soon thereafter the Japanese commander, General Saito Yoshitsugo, ordered a night banzai attack of 1,000 men led by sword-waving officers and thirty-six light tanks. Almost all died before the attack was recalled. The Japanese then fought stubbornly from mountain caves and foxholes, even though they had no chance of victory. When the end seemed near, General Saito ordered the most massive suicide attack yet seen in the Pacific. At dawn, over 4,000 officers and men, some so badly wounded they could barely hobble forward on crutches, threw themselves screaming into American machine-gun fire. When all had been killed, bulldozers buried the bodies in a mass grave. Many civilians, along with some Japanese soldiers, hid in caves in the rocky north end of the island. Convinced that the Americans would kill them if they surrendered, many killed themselves with hand grenades, others jumped off 800-foot cliffs to the rocks below, and still others swam out to sea with their infants.

agreed-upon Allied strategy ultimately called for MacArthur's forces to invade Leyte in the central Philippines on October 20, with fleet elements of Nimitz's command in support.

Although Japan's war leaders were still far from conceding defeat, it was becoming increasingly clear even to the most dogged nationalist that any hope of ultimate victory over the Allies was fast slipping away. Immediately following their devastating losses in the Marianas, Japanese strategists began anticipating an American assault somewhere in the Philippines. Expressing the Japanese view as to the strategic significance of the Philippines, Lieutenant General Shuichi Miyazaki, chief of the Operations Section at Imperial General Headquarters, declared:

Viewed from the standpoint of political and operational strategy, holding the Philippines was the one essential for the execution of the war against America and Britain. . . . The loss of the Philippines would greatly appropriate strategic bases for the enemy advance on Japan. If they were captured the advantage would be two to one in favor of the enemy and the prosecution of the war would suddenly take a great leap forward for the enemy.[32]

Notwithstanding the importance of the Philippines, however, the Japanese could not discount the possibility that the Americans might bypass the Philippines and launch a preemptive strike at any one of the southern, central, or northern Japanese home islands. To defend against any one of four attack possibilities, Japan's war planners drew up a fourfold contingency plan under the code name *Sho* (Japanese for "victory" or "to conquer"). The contingencies were labeled *Sho*-1 through *Sho*-4 and differed little except for the locale of their projected implementation.

All versions of the *Sho* plan were calculated to bring about the "decisive battle" that had been part and parcel of Japan's naval strategy since the Battle of Midway; and no matter where the battle might take place, all available forces were to be rushed to a "theater of decisive action."[33]

An Earnest Request

During a meeting attended by Emperor Hirohito in August, the Supreme War Direction Council decided that the Philippines were the next most likely American objective and that maximum forces should be deployed there. Their decision was validated two months later by information leaked by the Soviet Union—ostensibly an ally of the United States—through their foreign office in Moscow.

U.S. president Franklin D. Roosevelt (center, hands folded) and British prime minister Winston Churchill (center, holding cigar) meet in Quebec to discuss strategy against Japan.

On October 6, the Soviets informed the Japanese ambassador that the U.S. Fourteenth and Twentieth Army Air Forces, then China based, had received orders to start planning operations intended to isolate the Philippines. (The Soviet Union and Japan were then not yet at war.) The Soviet breach of faith removed all doubt as to the next American objective. Preparations to implement *Sho*-1 commenced at once. The Philippines would provide the locale for Japan's "Final Decisive Battle both on land and sea."[34] Caught in the fast-receding tide of Japan's declining empire, Japanese naval

warlords resorted to desperate—*suicidal*—measures.

On October 18, at a combined army-navy meeting, the staff of Admiral Soemu Toyoda, commander in chief of the Japanese Combined Fleet, informed attendees that an order to execute plan *Sho Ichi Go* (Operation Victory One, or *Sho*-1) had been issued the day before. Toyoda

Out of fuel, the Japanese cruiser Tone *could not avoid the inglorious fate of being sunk at anchor by U.S. planes.*

knew that many of his ships would be lost because of the minimal air support available to his naval forces and had already so informed the emperor. He emphasized that it was better to lose the ships in glorious action against the enemy now than to deactivate them in port later for lack of fuel. The navy was committed to a last-ditch effort to thwart the American invasion of the Philippines.

General Kenyro Sato, chief of the War Ministry's influential Military Affairs Bureau, suggested that it might be unwise to waste vessels in the Philippines that later might be vital to the defense of Japan's home islands. "Only the existence of the fleet will make the enemy cautious," he warned. "So, please, gentlemen, be prudent." [35]

Rear Admiral Tasuku Nakazawa, chief of the navy's Operations Section, countered by pointing out that the *Sho*-1 operation might be the Imperial Navy's last chance to die an honorable death. He called the Philippines "a fitting place to die." [36] With tears glistening in his dark eyes, he pleaded to a hushed room, "Please give the Combined Fleet the chance to bloom as flowers of death. This is the navy's earnest request." [37]

Chapter 3

Genesis in the Philippines

"The soldier and sailor should esteem valor. Ever since the ancient times valor has in our country been held in high esteem, and without it our subjects would be unworthy of their names."

—from the "Imperial Rescript to Soldiers and Sailors"

With the activation of *Sho*-1 on October 17, four separate battle groups of the Combined Fleet sailed from different locales and set course for the Philippines, there to execute a part of Admiral Toyoda's grandly impressive but highly complex battle plan.

Japan's major naval units—would slice through the San Bernardino Strait between

---

The Japanese hoped to lure Admiral William "Bull" Halsey's (pictured) fleet away from Leyte Gulf so that American amphibious forces could be isolated and destroyed.

The *Sho*-1 Plan

Basically, the plan called for Vice Admiral Jisaburo Ozawa's northern force, consisting largely of empty carriers, to lure Admiral William "Bull" Halsey's U.S. Third Fleet away from Leyte Gulf. Meanwhile, Vice Admiral Takeo Kurita's Singapore-based central force—then comprising some 60 percent of

Luzon and Samar and steam down into Leyte Gulf from the north. At the same time, Vice Admiral Shoji Nishimura's smaller southern force from Borneo and Malaya, reinforced by Vice Admiral Kiyohide Shima's attack force from the Ryukyu Islands, was to sail east and southeast through the Surigao Strait between Mindanao and Leyte. The central and southern forces would thus form a pincer in which to entrap and destroy all U.S. amphibious forces at sea and maroon all troops already ashore. The *Sho*-1 plan looked better on paper than it did during its execution.

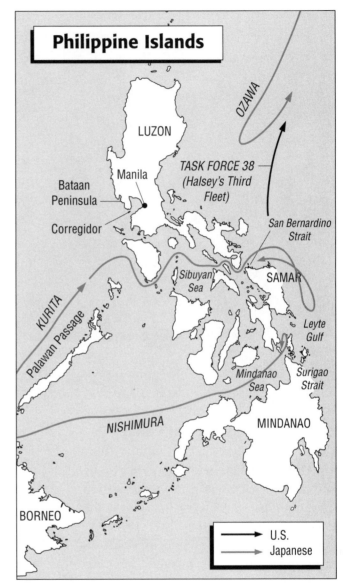

MacArthur Returns

On that same day, General Douglas MacArthur's amphibious forces stormed ashore at Leyte, in the central Philippines. After the Japanese had forced his evacuation from Corregidor Island on March 11, 1942, MacArthur issued a statement upon his arrival in Darwin, Australia, vowing, "I came through and I shall return." [38] Thirty-one months and nine days later, the charismatic old warrior waded onto the Leyte beach of Palo.

On October 20, 1944, in a sudden monsoon downpour, MacArthur addressed a crowd of elated Filipinos on hand to greet him. Speaking through a truck-mounted public-address system, his voice boomed out this message: "This is the Voice of Freedom, General MacArthur speaking. People of the Philippines: I have returned!" [39] The general had kept his promise.

Suicide as Official Policy

Earlier on October 17, Vice Admiral Takijiro Onishi (or Ohnishi) responded to the latest American threat. Onishi, an aviation specialist who had favorably assessed the Pearl Harbor attack plan three years earlier, flew into Nichols Field near Manila to take command of the Japanese First Air Fleet. A pilot himself and an officer of impeccable qualifications, he had most recently been in charge of aircraft production in the Aviation Department of the Ministry of Munitions in Tokyo. His reassignment foretold of an ominous shift in Japanese strategy.

Fulfilling the promise he made when he was forced to leave Corregidor, General Douglas MacArthur returns to the Phillipines on October 20, 1944.

On October 19, Admiral Onishi and his aide motored to Mabalacat airfield, a part of the sprawling Clark Field complex, about fifty miles north of Manila. The admiral wanted to lose no time in carrying out a radical plan that had preoccupied him for several months. Shortly after his arrival at the headquarters of the 201st Air Group in the late afternoon, he convened a quickly arranged meeting with the following key officers: Captain Rikihei Inoguchi, senior staff officer of the First Air Fleet; Commander Asaichi Tamai, executive officer of the 201st Air Group; Staff Officer Chuichi Yoshioka, of the Twenty-sixth Air Flotilla; and Lieutenants Masanobu Ibusuki and Ryo Yokoyama, squadron leaders of the 201st Air Group.

In the dim light of a single overhead lightbulb hanging by a wire, Onishi—usually lively and charismatic—appeared haggard and depressed. The message he bore weighed heavily on his soul:

In desperation, Admiral Takijiro Onishi (pictured) argued that the only way Japan could avoid defeat was through the use of kamikaze tactics.

As you know, the war situation is grave. The appearance of strong American forces in Leyte Gulf has been confirmed. The fate of the Empire depends upon the outcome of the *Sho* Operation, which Imperial General Headquarters has activated to hurl back the enemy assault on the Philippines. Our surface forces are already in motion. Vice Admiral Kurita's Second Fleet, containing our main battle strength, will advance to the Leyte area and annihilate the enemy invasion force. The mission of the First Air Fleet is to provide land-based air cover for Admiral Kurita's advance and make sure that enemy air attacks do not prevent him from reaching Leyte Gulf. To do this, we must hit the enemy's carriers and keep them neutralized for at least one week.

In my opinion, there is only one way of assuring that our meager strength will be effective to a maximum degree. That is to organize suicide attack units composed of

Zero fighters armed with 550-pound bombs, with each plane to crash-dive into an enemy carrier. . . . What do you think?[40]

Onishi paused to observe and evaluate the reactions of his junior officers. Japanese airmen had widely discussed the potential need for suicide flights during recent months.

Only four days earlier, in fact, Rear Admiral Masafumi Arima, commander of the Twenty-sixth Air Flotilla at Manila, had tried to crash his bomber into the U.S. carrier *Franklin*, east of Luzon. But Arima's failed effort was an unauthorized act of individual valor rather than an officially sanctioned suicide mission.

Until Onishi broached the issue as the new commander of the First Air Fleet, no one with high-command authority had proposed suicide flights as instruments of official policy. A hush came over the solemn gathering as each man contemplated both the personal and national ramifications of suicide as official policy.

When the admiral paused, all eyes turned toward Commander Tamai, who held the awesome responsibility for deciding the fate of his pilots. Tamai asked for a few minutes to confer in private with Lieutenant Ibusuki, one of his squadron leaders. Following a brief conversation, the two men rejoined the others. Tamai said: "I share completely the opinions expressed by the Admiral. The 201st Air group will carry out this proposal. May I ask that you

leave to us the organization of our crash-dive unit?"[41]

With Tamai's decision, a new and horrendous weapon was born: the *human bomb!* From this day forward, suicide flights would originate not from individual, spur-of-the-moment actions but from pre-planned, officially authorized assignments. Pilots who volunteered for these one-way flights would now have days, weeks, and, in some cases, months to contemplate their deaths.

The Weight of Duty

Once the admiral and his subordinates had agreed to go ahead with the unprecedented crash-dive tactic, the formation of special attack units became critically urgent. Four IJN attack forces were already steaming toward Leyte Gulf to engage and repulse the Americans. Since Onishi's task was to protect them from air attacks by crippling or sinking the American carriers off Leyte, the first flights of the new suicide units might come as early as the next day.

Commander Tamai, a father figure devoted to his pilots and their well-being, first consulted with his squadron leaders, then assembled all twenty-three of the air group's noncommissioned pilots. He painfully explained Admiral Onishi's proposal to them and asked for volunteers. All twenty-three pilots, veterans of the fighting over the Marianas, Yap, and Palau, raised their hands and affirmed the admiral's plan with expressions of joy and elation. They perhaps saw the proposed suicide missions as a way to avenge the deaths of fallen comrades.

Commander Tamai returned to the officers' quarters and spoke of his pilots' reactions. "Inoguchi," he said, "they are so young. But though they cannot explain what is in their hearts, I shall never forget the firm resolution in their faces."[42] And he did not. After the war Tamai became a Buddhist monk, convinced that he would never attain Nirvana (state of perfect blessedness) unless he soothed the souls of his subordinates "whom he killed in the Philippines."[43]

Once assured of enough volunteers to form crash-dive units, the selection of a

Kamikaze pilots plan their attack against U.S. ships. After Commander Tamai's decision, suicide missions would no longer be improvised acts.

leader for the first mission became the next matter of urgent concern. Inoguchi and Tamai agreed that the officer chosen for the task must be someone of superlative character and ability, preferably a graduate of the Naval Academy at Eta Jima. They considered these qualities essential both for ensuring a successful mission and for inspiring future crash-dive candidates. Lieutenant Yukio Seki, a recent transfer from Formosa (Taiwan), met the necessary requirements and was quickly selected. Tamai sent an orderly to waken and summon Seki at once.

Lieutenant Seki arrived in the officers' room on the ground floor of the headquarters building shortly after midnight, still buttoning his jacket and looking half asleep. Commander Tamai invited him to sit down and said, "Admiral Onishi has brought to our base the idea of loading Zero fighters with a 250-kg. [551-pound] bomb and having the pilots crash dive on enemy warships. I have recommended you as a proper man to lead such a task."[44]

The capable young naval officer, married only a few months earlier, leaned forward supporting his bowed head in his hands, with elbows planted on the table and eyes closed. Seki sat in silence for several seconds, his only movement the tightening of his clenched fists. Then he raised his head, combed back his long hair with his fingers, and spoke in scarcely more than a murmur. "You absolutely must let me do it,"[45] he said. The lieutenant had made the only choice expected of a graduate of the Naval Academy.

Seki rose and started to leave. Captain Inoguchi stopped him momentarily and asked his only question of the brief session. "You are still a bachelor, aren't you?"

"No," Seki replied, "I am married, sir."[46]

Tamai thanked Seki and bade him good night. The commander's eyes glistened with tears. Duty is weightier than a mountain.

The First Four

With the selection of an officer to lead the twenty-three enlisted volunteers, assigning a name to the new suicide corps was the only remaining question. Captain Inoguchi suggested *Shimpu* (or *Shinpu*), a variant interpretation of the Japanese characters for *kamikaze*. Tamai agreed, saying, "We need a man-made Kamikaze."[47]

The twenty-four members of the newly formed *Shimpu* Special Attack Corps (*Shimpu Tokubetsu-Kogekitai*) were then divided into four units, subsequently named *Shikishima* (Beautiful Island), *Yamato* (the Japanese people; also the old name for Japan), *Asahi* (Rising Sun), and *Yamazakura* (Wild Cherry Blossom). These four names were drawn from an ancient Japanese poem:

> If you ask me what is the soul of the
>   Japanese,
> The people of the Beautiful Island,
> I will tell you that it is the Wild Cherry
>   Blossom
> That scatters its perfume in the light
>   of the Rising Sun.[48]

"The Best Place in Death"

In October 1945, in Tokyo, U.S. officials interrogated Captain Rikihei Inoguchi, Imperial Japanese Navy chief of staff of the First Air Fleet during the Philippine campaign. Inoguchi's statements were extracted from U.S. naval records by Bertram Vogel, a World War II naval intelligence officer, and shown in his article "Who Were the Kamikaze?" (*U.S. Naval Institute Proceedings*, July 1947):

> Admiral Onishi ordered the organization of the Kamikaze on 19 October 1944. They were ready to go on 20 October, but no opportunity presented itself. On 25 October the first kamikaze attack was made, having a great morale-raising effect. Although the attacks were ordered by the Commander in Chief (1st Air Fleet), in fact it was originated by the feeling of all combatants in the Philippine area. . . .

> For example, on 15 October, Admiral Arima, Commander of the 26th Air Squadron, himself dove into an aircraft carrier. [Arima's attempt to crash-dive into the U.S. carrier *Franklin* fell short, and his bomber crashed into the sea.] Admiral Arima lit the fuse of the ardent wishes of his men in order to bring their wishes into reality. At this time we in the Philippines thought about the approach of the crisis, owing to the odds. So we felt as follows: we must give our lives to the Emperor and Country, this is our inborn feeling. I am afraid you cannot understand it well, or may call it desperate or foolish. We Japanese base our lives on obedience to Emperor and Country. On the other hand, we wish for the best place in death, according to Bushido. Kamikaze originates from these feelings. . . . It was the incarnation of these feelings.

"The blossom of the wild cherry, having scattered its perfume, falls without regrets," interprets surviving kamikaze pilot Ryuji Nagatsuka. "The meaning of this verse is that our people must always be ready to die for the benefit of their country, and, like the blossom, they must fall without regrets."[49]

In the early morning hours of October 20, 1944, Captain Inoguchi left Commander Tamai and trudged up the darkened stairs to Admiral Onishi's second-floor sleeping quarters to report on their progress. He found the admiral lying on a cot in the dark, unable to sleep, troubled by thoughts of Japan's fate and of how history might record his role in sending his nation's finest young men to a knowing death. Onishi arose, snapped on the light, and sat on his cot to hear Inoguchi's lengthy report.

"Since this is a special affair, we wish you to christen the unit," the captain concluded. "Commander Tamai and I suggest that it be called the *Shimpu* Unit."[50] Admiral Onishi nodded his approval and called for his aide. He then dictated the following order for immediate posting:

> The 201st Air Group will organize a special attack corps and will destroy or disable, if possible by October 25, the enemy carrier forces in the waters east of the Philippines.

> The corps will be called the *Shimpu* Attack Unit. It will consist of 26 fighter planes, of which half will be assigned to

crash-diving missions, and the remainder to escort, and will be divided into four sections, designated as follows: *Shikishima, Yamato, Asahi,* and *Yamazakura.*

The *Shimpu* Attack Unit will be commanded by Lieutenant Yukio Seki.[51]

Thus the first four groups of kamikazes became official, albeit short-lived, entities. History would not soon forget them.

Mixed Emotions

As might be expected, emotions ran high over the formation of the special attack squads. Perhaps no one felt the burden of their premise and performances more than Admiral Onishi, founder and father to them all. Before leaving Mabalacat on the morning of October 20, he stood before four ranks of six pilots and said:

Japan is in great danger. The salvation of our country is now beyond the powers of the ministers of state, the General Staff, and the lowly commanders like myself. It can come only from spirited young men such as you. Thus, on behalf of your one hundred million countrymen, I ask of you this sacrifice and pray for your success. You are already gods, without earthly desires. But one thing you want to know is that your own crash-dive is not in vain. Regrettably, we will not be able to tell you the results. But I shall watch your efforts to the end and re-

> ## Member of the Group
>
> Shortly after forming the first official kamikaze group at the airfield at Mabalacat, Luzon, Vice Admiral Takijiro Onishi sent a poem to the original volunteers, written in his own calligraphy (stylized characters). In *Kamikaze: Japan's Suicide Samurai,* Japanologist and historian Raymond Lamont-Brown reproduces and translates Onishi's message to his fledglings:
>
> *Kijo sakite, osu chiru*
> *Hana no wagami ka na*
> *Ikade sono ka wo*
> *Kiyoku todomen.*
>
> ("Blossoming today, tomorrow scattered / Life is like a delicate flower / Can one expect the fragrance to last forever?")
>
> The admiral signed it *Onishi Kamikaze Tokkotai Ei,* which means Onishi Kamikaze Special Attack Unit Member. "Not only was he their father," writes Lamont-Brown, "he was an *ei* (member) of the group."

port your deeds to the Throne. You may all rest assured on this point. I ask you all to do your best.[52]

Although the suicide units comprised volunteers, purportedly eager to sacrifice themselves for emperor and country, not every pilot accepted his fate with equanimity. A disapproving voice was in fact raised by Lieutenant Yukio Seki himself. Masashi Onoda, a war correspondent for the Japanese news agency *Domei,* joined Seki for a walking interview alongside the Bamban River at Mabalacat, soon after the formation of the *Shimpu* unit. According to Onoda, Seki told him:

Japan must be in very bad shape if it has to kill an experienced pilot like me. If they would let me, I could drop a 500-kilogram [1,102-pound] bomb on the flight deck of a carrier without going in for body-crashing and still make my way back. I am not going out tomorrow for the Japanese Emperor, but for my beloved [wife]. If Japan were defeated, who knows what the Americans would do to my wife [Mariko]. I am going to die to protect her.[53]

Starting on October 21, 1944, Lieutenant Seki and his *Shikishima* unit tried unsuccessfully on four consecutive days to make contact with the enemy fleet east of the Philippines. On their fifth attempt, they sighted Task Unit 77.4.3 (Taffy 3) of the U.S. Seventh Fleet. Seki and four companions plunged to their deaths. Battle accounts credit Seki and one other pilot with sinking the American escort carrier *St. Lo.* Seki's three other pilots severely damaged but did not sink three additional U.S. escort carriers.

Distorted Successes

Earlier that same morning, six kamikazes of the *Yamato* unit had already attacked warships of Taffy 1 (Task Unit 77.4.1) north of Mindanao, about seventy miles to the south. Taffy 1, commanded by Rear Admiral

Thomas L. Sprague (no relation to Taffy 3's commander), comprised four escort carriers and eight destroyers. The *Yamato* pilots, flying out of an airfield in Cebu, commenced their attack at 0740 on October 25.

The first bomb-laden Zeke (Zero) crashed into the *Santee*, a CVE. Another Zeke struck a second CVE, the *Suwanee*. American gunners blasted three Zekes out of the air, and a sixth disappeared in the clouds and was not heard from again. Damage control parties patched up the two damaged carriers and flight operations resumed in short order.

The Suwanee *is set afire after being hit by a Zeke. The flames were quickly extinguished, and the carrier was soon back in action.*

Antiaircraft gun crews aboard the ships of Taffy 1 shot down three kamikazes on October 25, 1944. The worst was yet to come.

The commanding officer of the *Petrof Bay*, a third CVE, scoffed at the new suicide tactic, noting that it "is a stupid way to attack *because it has less chance of getting home* than other types of bombing."[54] Besides offering a larger target, he argued, the aircraft had less penetrating power than a bomb. But this was only the beginning.

Nonetheless, the American skipper's criticism contained much merit. The first kamikazes had died courageously but without neutralizing the American carriers.

Rather than winning a decisive battle in Leyte Gulf, the Imperial Navy suffered a huge defeat. But embellished reports of the initial kamikaze successes would soon help to persuade Admiral Onishi that a broader application of suicidal tactics was essential to Japan's survival.

Chapter 4

Expanding Kamikaze Operations

"Faithfulness and righteousness are the ordinary duties of a man, but the soldier and sailor, in particular, cannot be without them and remain in the ranks even for a day. . . . If you thoughtlessly agree to do something that is vague in its nature, and bind yourself to unwise obligations, and then try to prove yourself faithful and righteous, you may find yourself in great straits from which there is no escape."

—from the "Imperial Rescript to Soldiers and Sailors"

On October 23, 1944, under orders from Admiral Soemu Toyoda, the 350 aircraft of the Japanese Second Air Fleet arrived at Clark Field. Admiral Toyoda had directed its commander, Vice Admiral Shigeru Fukudome, to coordinate operations closely with the First Air Fleet.

A Unified Command

Over the next three days, Admiral Onishi met with Fukudome several times in an effort to persuade him to join the First Air Fleet in some of its special attacks. Onishi began by apprising Fukudome of First Air Fleet's critical situation:

The First Air Fleet has been terribly shot up during the past month. It has fewer than 50 planes actually available for combat. There are about 30 fighters, and only a few bombers ("Betty"), *Tenzan* torpedo bombers ("Jill"), and *Suisei* carrier bombers ("Judy"). [The Japanese customarily assigned male names to fighters and female names to bombers.]

With so few planes it is impossible for us to continue fighting by conventional tactics. To do so would just wipe out our remaining strength. In view of this situation, and after a full examination

51

Despite pressure from Admiral Onishi, Vice Admiral Shigeru Fukudome (seated, at left) was extremely reluctant to resort to kamikaze attacks.

are trained for, but their effectiveness in this situation is very doubtful. We firmly believe that the First Air Fleet's special attacks will bring about the desired results. We wish you to share some of your fighters with us.[55]

Fukudome's ears remained closed to Onishi's arguments. But on the night of October 26—following two ineffectual mass air attacks by the Second Air Fleet on October 24 and 25 and a relatively highly effective special attack by the First Air Fleet's *Shikishima* unit, Onishi again implored Fukudome to join him in special attacks: "The evidence is quite conclusive that special attacks are our only chance. In this critical situation we must not lose precious time. It is imperative that the Second Air Fleet agree to special attacks."[56]

and investigation of the various possibilities, First Air Fleet has decided upon special attacks as offering the only chance of success. It is my hope that Second Air Fleet will join us in these attacks.

But Fukudome, former chief of the Operations Bureau of the Naval General Staff, strongly favored conventional air attacks. Onishi tried a different approach that evening:

I am not in a position to deny the value of mass-formation attacks such as you

Fukudome expressed concerns about the potentially damaging effect on the morale of his pilots. But Onishi, after long hours of persuasion, convinced him that pilot morale would not become a problem. Reluctantly, Fukudome agreed to adopt kamikaze tactics, and the two admirals agreed to unite their air fleets under Fukudome, the ranking officer, with Onishi as his chief of staff. Their unified command—named the Combined Land-based Air Force—constituted the first step in extending the kamikaze operations.

Onishi's Reasoning

Ironically, the modest success of the *Shikishima* group—commanded by Lieutenant Yukio Seki, who privately opposed the use of suicide weapons—led to a rapid increase in the use of the very tactics Seki deplored. Admiral Onishi, of course, spearheaded the expansion of kamikaze operations. Other high-command officers eventually endorsed and assumed leadership of massive suicide attacks later, but it was Onishi's driving force behind the movement in the early going that earned him the title of *Otosama no kamikaze* (Father of the Divine Wind).[57]

Over the course of his naval career, Onishi had developed a reputation among his peers as something of a maverick. His short, stocky figure, close-cropped hair, protruding ears, big nose, steely eyes, and often outspoken demeanor underscored his qualities of courage, intelligence, and aggressive character. He scorned incompetence and was quick to admonish its presence in his peers or subordinates. One of Japan's earliest aviation advocates and foremost aviation authorities, he graduated seventh in his class from the Naval Academy at Eta Jima in 1912.

Onishi rose steadily in rank over the next two decades, despite an untoward incident in which he slapped a geisha (a skilled female entertainer and witty conversationalist) and was charged with conduct unbecoming an officer. He was appointed rear

Constraining Circumstances

Six years after World War II, surviving kamikaze Ryuji Nagatsuka questioned Vice Admiral Shigeru Fukudome, former commander of the Japanese Second Air Fleet, about the admiral's own suicide-attack groups. In *I Was a Kamikaze*, Nagatsuka shares Fukudome's reply:

> At that period, I was sharing a room in the headquarters of Two Hundred and First Squadron with Vice Admiral Onishi. He kept repeating that there was no other mode of action still open to us, and urged me to form similar corps in the Naval Air Fleet, which, by then, was nonexistent except on paper. . . . Having no aircraft carriers left, we were perforce [by necessity] land-based. . . . But the fact was, my pilots were terribly inexperienced. En route for Clark Field, we attacked the U.S. Task Force off the coast of Formosa [Taiwan], and some of my pilots mistook dolphins for enemy submarines. . . . On the twenty-fourth and twenty-fifth of October, we attacked the Task Force with all the means at our disposal. Result: two cruisers and three destroyers damaged. Need I say more?
>
> On the other hand, on the twenty-fifth, the *Shikishima* group carried off a brilliant success, sinking two ships, including the aircraft carrier *Saint Lo.* [Actually, only the *St. Lo* was sunk by the *Shikishima* group.] I spent the night of the twenty-fifth—twenty-six arguing with Onishi and finally promised him the support of all my Zeros. At dawn, I interrogated my staff officers. Some said this was now the only possible form of attack, others insisted we should try one more large-scale conventional attack. However, it had been drizzling since morning and in these conditions it would have been difficult to maintain flying formations. It was, therefore, circumstances that constrained me to take the final decision: I opted for special suicide-missions.

Mission Impossible

An impossible task greeted Vice Admiral Takijiro Onishi's return to the Philippines in October 1944. In *Zero!* Masatake Okumiya and Jiro Horikoshi (with Martin Caidin) explain:

> He returned to the battlefield where once he had led the attack, only this time his opponents thundered toward the Philippines with the greatest massed carrier air power in history. . . .

> Vice Admiral Onishi's hands were literally tied before he made his first official move. Not only were his fighter planes primarily the all-too-familiar Zero [by then obsolescent], but he could not scrape together from every field in the Philippines more than thirty serviceable fighters. By patching up every remaining Type 1 Betty bomber on the islands, he managed to increase his defensive force of operational aircraft to a pitiful total of only sixty planes. Onishi realized the futility of his task: not even by the wildest stretch of the imagination could he hope to inflict heavy damage upon or to destroy the American carriers so well guarded by the Hellcat fighter planes. Without fighter-plane escort, Onishi mused, even the mighty battleships *Yamato* and *Musashi,* despite their eighteen-inch guns and slabs of armor plating, would be destroyed by American carrier bombers long before they would have the opportunity to even *see* the enemy fleet, let alone engage it in combat.

> Since orthodox methods of attack could no longer be pursued to carry out his mission, Onishi turned to the possibility of *Kamikaze* attacks—suicide dive bombing with Zero fighters carrying 550-pound bombs.

American aircraft carriers advance with their decks filled with bombers and fighter planes. Conventional tactics against such an armada would be futile.

admiral in 1939, and in early 1941 he participated in a study to determine the feasibility of an air attack on Pearl Harbor.

At the outbreak of World War II, while serving as chief of staff, Eleventh Air Fleet, Onishi directed a series of devastating air attacks on U.S. bases in the Philippines. He was appointed vice admiral just prior to assuming command of the First Air Fleet in October 1944.

An unflagging patriot and consummate man of action, Onishi's soft, flabby exterior tended to belie his inner toughness. "He favored men who could be counted on to put words into deeds," noted Captain Rikihei Inoguchi, his senior staff officer in the Philippines. "He was opposed to men who merely talked and argued on paper without accomplishing anything. In talking with him, one always had the feeling that his penetrating gaze was fathoming one's innermost thoughts."[58] In short, in his role as creator of the kamikaze corps, Vice Admiral Takijiro Onishi was the right man for the job at the right time and place.

Onishi's inspiration for creating his unique corps of death divers issued from a variety of sources too numerous to cite, but doubtlessly the thinking of Captain Eiichiro Jyo (sometimes Jo or Iyo) influenced him greatly. Jyo—a former naval attaché in Washington and naval aide-de-camp to Emperor Hirohito, and later the captain of the light carrier *Chiyoda*—was among the first to acknowledge and to seek a means of countering the enemy's superior naval air strength.

In June 1944, after the Battle of the Philippine Sea, Jyo analyzed Japan's fighting strength compared to their enemy's and submitted a radical proposal to his superiors:

No longer can we hope to sink the numerically superior enemy aircraft carriers through ordinary attack methods. I urge the immediate organiza-

tion of special attack units to carry out crash-dive tactics, and I ask to be placed in command of them.[59]

Onishi—then serving as chief of the General Affairs Bureau of the Aviation Department in the Ministry of Munitions—knew firsthand of Japan's failure to keep pace with U.S. aircraft production and foresaw a grim future for his country. At first, he opposed suicide tactics as not only inhumane but wasteful of both pilots and planes. But a combination of factors soon changed his thinking.

Bomber nose assemblies take shape on an American production line. Japan had no way of matching the industrial might of the United States.

Zero fighters litter an airfield after being destroyed on the ground by U.S. aircraft. Plans to reinforce Onishi's First Air Fleet were decimated by this setback.

Defective aircraft unsuitable for most combat situations were pouring off Japanese assembly lines, which were worked by children of high school age and younger. Accelerated flight-training programs were churning out fledglings barely capable of taking off and landing their airplanes, let alone pilots able to match the air-fighting skills of their enemy. A fuel shortage gripped Japan. And Japanese air strength had fallen off sharply under enemy guns.

During a three-day attack on Formosa, beginning October 12 U.S. fighters and bombers destroyed a fleet of Japanese air-craft slated to reinforce Onishi's First Air Fleet in the Philippines. Admiral Fukudome, Second Air Fleet commander, later reported that more than five hundred of his aircraft had been shot down like "so many eggs thrown against the stone wall of indomitable enemy formations." [60]

Above all, Onishi reasoned, a stirring Japanese victory was desperately needed to boost the sagging morale both at the front and at home. In light of all these factors, the crash-dive tactics proposed by Captain Jyo took on a new appeal for the fifty-four-year-old patriot. Onishi explains:

> Several months ago when Captain Jyo kept insisting on this kind of attack, I was loathe to accept his idea. But when I came to the Philippines and saw the actual state of affairs, it was clear that these tactics would have to be adopted.[61]

Coincidentally, in the continuing irony of war, Jyo went down with his ship in Leyte Gulf on October 25—the date of the first successful kamikaze attack.

Reassessing Japan's Strategy

On October 30, 1944, Admiral Mitsumasa Yonai—the large, brusque Japanese navy minister—informed Emperor Hirohito of the initial kamikaze successes in Leyte Gulf. Hirohito responded curiously. "Was it necessary to go to this extreme?" he asked, adding, "The men certainly did a magnificent job."[62]

In the Philippines, Admiral Onishi interpreted the emperor's comments as implied criticism of his decision to initiate suicidal tactics. He or-

dered his commanders to read the emperor's remarks to all surviving kamikazes, adding: "His Majesty's words suggest that His Majesty is greatly concerned. We must redouble our efforts to relieve His Majesty of this concern. I have pledged our every effort to that end."[63] Most informed sources agree that Onishi had originally intended to conduct the suicide flights for *one week only*—and only in support of the Imperial Japanese Navy's "decisive battle" in Philippine waters. But that was before the IJN's epic defeat in the

Emperor Hirohito is seen here in the royal limousine. His response to the news of the first kamikaze attacks was interpreted as a desire to increase the effort.

A Japanese heavy cruiser maneuvers desperately to avoid bombs dropped by U.S. planes over Leyte Gulf. Japan lost 29 warships in the battle.

Battle of Leyte Gulf, in which the IJN lost 4 carriers, 3 battleships, 6 heavy and 4 light cruisers, 11 destroyers, a submarine, about 500 aircraft, and some 10,500 sailors and airmen killed in action.

In the battle's aftermath, Vice Admiral Takijiro Onishi, the maverick founder and father of the kamikazes, reassessed Japan's fading strategic fortunes and felt duty bound not only to continue kamikaze operations but to expand them.

Chapter 5

The Kamikazes

"The soldier and sailor should make simplicity their aim. If you do not make simplicity your aim, you will . . . grow selfish and sordid and sink to the last degree of baseness, so that neither loyalty nor valor will avail to save you from the contempt of the world."

—from the "Imperial Rescript to Soldiers and Sailors"

T he end of October 1944 witnessed the last of the original *Shimpu* unit volunteers, but their limited success touched off a wave of enthusiasm sufficient to justify—even to mandate—the continuance and expansion of kamikaze operations. Some sources maintain that Admiral Onishi had never really intended to limit body-crashing tactics to only one week in support of *Sho*-1. Irrespective of the admiral's original intent, however, any official thought of discontinuing suicide flights abruptly disappeared in a torrent of new volunteers.

"The enthusiasm spread out to all ranks and rates of Army and Navy fliers and brought volunteers far in excess of available planes," writes Roger Pineau, former naval officer, author, and collaborator on the authoritative *History of United States*

Seconds before impact, a U.S. cruiser tries to blast a kamikaze off course. The limited success of the first suicide missions brought an outpouring of new volunteers.

Naval Operations in World War II. "It spread upward to Imperial General Headquarters and brought no objection to the continuation and expansion of the suicide effort." [64] With tacit approval of the kamikazes at the highest level, Japan's last hope of salvaging victory from an all but inevitable defeat was blowing on the wind for the rest of the war—the Divine Wind.

At this point, a brief look at the indoctrination, training, tactics, aircraft, and attitudes of the kamikazes might further a deeper understanding of their unique role in history.

Indoctrination and Training

Japan had gambled away most of its navy in the Battle of Leyte Gulf but failed to halt the American advance in the Philippines.

Diving through a curtain of antiaircraft fire, a kamikaze zeroes in on the Lexington *during the Battle of Leyte Gulf. Moments later the pilot hit his target.*

Within twenty-four hours after Admirals Fukudome and Onishi combined forces, seven new special attack units were formed. The kamikaze mission was changed to flying sorties (a sortie equals one flight by a single military plane) in support of Japanese ground troops, striking at American transports and cargo ships carrying troop reinforcements and supplies.

As the American foothold on Leyte grew stronger, the Japanese situation grew more desperate by the day and the volume and intensity of kamikaze attacks increased in direct proportion to Japanese desperation. The frenzied activity quickly depleted the serviceable aircraft available in the Philippines. Admiral Onishi flew to Tokyo in November and pleaded with the high command for three hundred more planes for kamikaze operations. They granted him half that number.

Although kamikaze volunteers abounded, experienced pilots did not. This led to special indoctrination courses on Formosa, where two schools were established for pilot training. Captain Rikihei Inoguchi, Admiral Onishi's chief of staff in the Philippines, established the training regimen and later summarized it this way:

The indoctrination for the new Kamikaze pilots lasted seven days. The first two days were spent exclusively in take-off practice. This covered the time from the moment the order to sortie was given until the planes of a unit were airborne and assembled. During the next two days, lessons were devoted to formation flying, with a continuation of interest in take-off practice. The last three days were given primarily to the study and practice of approaching and attacking the target. But here, again, take-off and formation practice were included. Had time permitted, this whole schedule would have been run through a second time.[65]

Clearly, the program outlined by Captain Inoguchi devoted a lot of time to takeoff practice and with good reason. Taking off with a 550-pound bomb attached to the aircraft required great caution. If a pilot lifted off the ground in the usual way, he might cause his aircraft to stall, with disastrous results. Accordingly, dummy weights, such as logs, were affixed to the planes during practice.

Since the success of any kamikaze mission depended upon the pilot's ability to reach and strike his target, fledgling and experienced pilots alike spent the remainder of their seven-day indoctrination training practicing formation flying and tactics.

Formation Flying and Tactics

During kamikaze operations over Leyte Gulf, certain attack methods proved superior to others in their effectiveness and gave rise to new formations and procedures. Tacticians decided on a standard five-plane attack formation comprising three crash-dive aircraft and two escorts.

Small groups offered maximum mobility and stood a better chance of reaching

A suicide pilot misses his target and falls harmlessly into the ocean. Successful kamikaze attacks depended on skills learned during seven-day indoctrination courses.

their targets than larger formations. Smaller groups of aircraft held an added advantage in that they could be more easily hidden under trees and foliage adjacent to Philippine airfields subject to frequent U.S. attacks. Later, they could be more readily returned to their often distant runways.

The more experienced pilots flew escort, one above and one below the attack planes. It took great skill to fly escort, and the role was critical to the success of a mission. "Escort pilots had to be able to dodge adroitly and bluff the enemy, rather than just shoot him down," notes Commander Tadashi Nakajima, Admiral Onishi's operations officer. "An escort pilot's first duty was to shield the suicide planes in his mission, even if it meant the sacrifice of his own life."[66]

Although the three-two formation became standard practice in kamikaze operations, its use was by no means mandatory. As in most (if not all) military applications, tactics varied to fit the time, place, and situation. (Tactics and strategy are sometimes confused. Briefly, the term *tactics* defines the art of placing or maneuvering forces skillfully in a battle, whereas *strategy* represents the plan for an entire operation of a war or campaign.) The kamikazes—flying such light and swift airplanes as the Zero fighter (Zeke) or the *Suisei* carrier bomber (Judy) in the earlier operations—developed two methods (or tactics) for approaching and attacking their targets: high level and ground level.

Pilots were free to select whichever method they preferred. Those choosing the high-level approach generally flew at altitudes of 19,000 to 23,000 feet. Although a high-level approach allowed American radar to detect their presence at long ranges, U.S. fighters took a long time climbing to such great heights and could be seen coming. Pilots opting for a low-level approach could expect to escape radar

At the end of a steep dive, this kamikaze crashed into the side of the battleship Missouri *but failed to put the ship out of action.*

detection flying at wave-top heights until they drew within ten miles of their target. Also, U.S. fighters flying routine Combat Air Patrols (CAPs) had difficulty spotting intruders skimming along the wave tops.

A medium-altitude approach afforded the advantage of better navigational accuracy and range of visibility, but easier detection and interception quickly ruled out a midlevel approach. When sufficient aircraft were available, both high- and low-level approaches were used, along with diverse routes to targets.

Target Selection

Suicide pilots were instructed to concentrate their efforts on the most valuable targets wherever possible. Enemy carriers generally represented their prime targets, followed by battleships, heavy and light cruisers, destroyers, and so on.

To either sink or render a warship inoperational, pilots aimed for the ship's most vulnerable points—in the case of a carrier, the central elevator, followed by either the fore or aft elevator. Battleships and cruisers were most vulnerable at their nerve center located at the base of the bridge. Against smaller warships and transports, a direct hit almost anywhere between the bridge and the center of the ship was usually fatal.

In theory, four planes were needed to sink or disable a large carrier—two to strike its central elevator and one each impacting its fore and aft elevators. Two or three attackers were considered ideal for taking out an escort carrier. In the real world, however, the Americans had too many carriers and the Japanese too few planes to test the validity of such theoretical ideals. Targets were usually selected at random, and synchronized attacks occurred only rarely and then mostly by chance.

Commander Arthur M. Purdy—skipper of the U.S. destroyer *Abner Reed*, sunk by kamikazes in Philippine waters—later marveled at the enemy's seeming lack of coordination:

> There appeared to be no special tactics used during the approach of these planes. Each bomber seemed to be very much on his own and it was up to him to pick his target and make his attack. His one mission, of course, is to get in and get aboard.[67]

Nothing was more critical in determining whether a kamikaze pilot would "get in and get aboard" than his angle of attack.

Angle of Attack

Pilots who elected to fly a high-altitude approach were taught to make a long shallow dive on target, while keeping track of wind direction and dive velocity. Too steep a dive might result in too much speed and cause the pilot to veer off target or even to lose control of his aircraft. "At the end of the trajectory, the nose of the plane had to be pulled up to an angle of forty-five to fifty-five degrees in relation to the point aimed at," writes former kamikaze Ryuji Nagatsuka, who trained for a crash dive but never had to make it. "There could be only one

Coming in at too steep an angle and too great a speed, a kamikaze loses control of his aircraft and veers from the target, the carrier Sangamon.

attempt at this approach."[68] Failure to hit the target meant one more useless death.

Attackers flying a low-altitude approach were instructed to climb quickly to about fifteen hundred feet upon sighting their target before commencing a steep dive on target. This method required considerable piloting skill to ensure a steep downward plunge for maximum effectiveness.

Since the death of the pilot was already conceded, all that remained was for him to make his death count for something. His choice of approaches offered him little as-

surance of success, in either case, as the following admonitions from one of Ryuji Nagatsuka's flight instructors implies:

If you are shot down during your crash-dive, you will die in vain. In the case of a water-skimming approach, you run the risk of being caught in water spouts [thrown up by exploding shells], as well as by ack-ack [antiaircraft fire]. If you use the high-altitude approach, enemy fighters may shoot you down. Success is, either way, problematic.[69]

At the onset of kamikaze attacks, the aircraft used comprised some of Japan's best—the Zekes and the Judys and others. But as the war dragged on and the numbers and quality of Japanese planes dwindled and deteriorated, any serviceable aircraft was considered fit for kamikaze action. Success became even more "problematic."

Kamikaze Aircraft

Between 1941 and 1945, the Japanese produced some fifty thousand fighters, bombers, and aircraft and an additional twenty thousand transports and trainers. Many of these were pressed into service with special attack units during the last ten months of the war, including heavy bombers, flying boats, and intermediate trainers. Swift single-engine fighters and speedy light bombers held sway as the preferred kamikaze aircraft.

Preeminent among all of the aircraft used was the Mitsubishi A6M Zero fighter (the *Reisen*, or Zero-Sen), code-named Zeke by the Allies. (The Allies assigned code names to all Japanese planes to aid rapid identification and cut down on lengthy combat reports.) By far the most famous and widely used Japanese aircraft

of the war, the Zero was produced in a succession of model changes. Most models had reached obsolescence by 1943, however, and were later modified to carry heavier bombs and assigned to kamikaze units.

Five aircraft carried the brunt of the kamikaze attacks in the bomber class: Mitsubishi G4M (Navy Type 97) torpedo bomber, code-named Betty; Mitsubishi Ki-67 *Hiryu* (Flying Dragon) standard bomber, code-named Peggy; Nakajima B6N *Tenzan* (Heavenly Mountain) carrier attack plane and torpedo bomber, code-named Jill; Yokosuka D4Y *Suisei* (Comet) carrier-based bomber converted to a catapult-launched dive-bomber, code-named Judy; and the Yokosuka P4Y1 *Ginga* (Milky Way) twin-engine land-based bomber adapted for use as a night fighter, code-named Frances. All of these aircraft were modified as needed to enhance their use

The Mitsubishi A6M Zero-Sen fighter was the aircraft used most often in kamikaze attacks. Almost unbeatable at the start of the war, the type was obsolete by 1943.

Two other types of planes used by the divine wind were the Mitsubishi G4M bomber (above) and the Nakajima B6N Tenzan (here a captured B6N is being test flown in U.S. markings).

in crash-dive applications, primarily to carry heavier bomb loads and to eliminate the usual bomb-release mechanism.

While these modified conventional aircraft were pioneering kamikaze attacks in the Philippines, Japanese engineers were developing a more unconventional rocket-powered, bomb-delivery system in Japan. The Japanese, with their traditional flair for poetics, called it the *Ohka* (Cherry Blossom); the Americans, less lyrically, called it the *baka* bomb—the "foolish" or "stupid" bomb.

Cherry Blossoms and Thunder Gods

The *Ohka* (spelled *Oka* and translated as "Exploding Cherry Blossom" by some sources) was a small glider about 20 feet long, with stubby wings spanning 16 feet 5

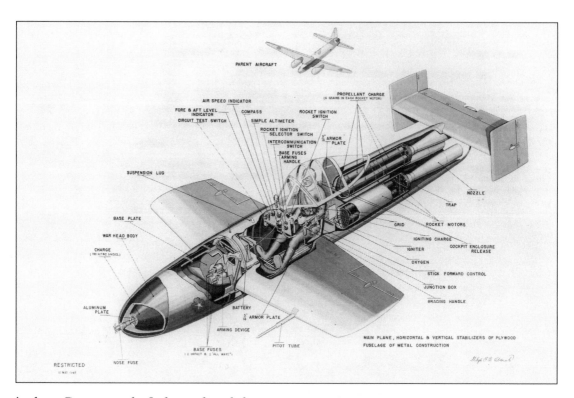

This diagram shows the layout of the Ohka rocket-assisted flying bomb. The weapon was carried aloft by a mother plane and released once near its target.

inches. Constructed of plywood and dura-lumin (a light aluminum alloy), it carried three rocket boosters in its tail and 2,645 pounds of explosives in its nose. The *Ohka* was essentially a flying bomb guided by a single pilot, capable of reaching speeds of 525 MPH in level flight and 625 MPH in its final dive.

The *Ohka* lacked wheels and had a limited range of about fifty-five miles. Thus, it had to be affixed to the underside of a mother plane (a modified Mitsubishi G4M Betty) and airlifted to the general target area. The *Ohka* pilot rode in the mother plane until the target was sighted, then transferred through the bomb bay of the Betty into the tiny cockpit of the flying bomb. About twenty or thirty miles from the target, the *Ohka* was released from the mother plane by a triggering mechanism, at a height of no less than fifteen thousand feet. The *Ohka* pilot then fired his first rocket and began gliding toward his target—and eternity.

Credit for the design of the awesome rocket plane goes to Special Service Sub-lieutenant Shoichi Ohta (or Ota), attached to the 1081st Naval Flying Corps. He conceived the idea for a piloted bomb in 1943, and work began on a prototype in the spring of 1944. Production started on October 1. By March 1945 a total of 755 *Ohka* in various models were built, but the only model to see operational service was the Navy Suicide Attacker *Ohka* Model 11 (Yokosuka MXY7).

Recruiting posters seeking volunteer pilots for the *Ohka*s began appearing in Japan and at Japanese bases overseas in August 1944. On October 1, 1944, the *Jinrai Butai* (Thunder Gods Special Attack Corps) was formed and officially designated the 721st Naval Flying Corps. Thus historically, both in concept and spirit, they predated Admiral Onishi's original *Shimpu* unit.

Although kamikazes in the purest sense, the Thunder Gods stood apart from their peers in conventional aircraft in that they spent six months learning to fly the *Ohka*s and preparing to die. Commander Tadashi Nakajima writes:

> In a moment of sudden emergency it is not so difficult to make up one's mind to die. But it must have been agony for the young men who were chosen to train and study for *Ohka* special attacks, because it was more than six months after the training started before even the first of them got a chance to die in battle.[70]

Their first opportunity to die came on March 21, 1945, on a mission against an American task force off Okinawa, a mission destined to fail totally. A Japanese formation of 18 Bettys (16 carrying *Ohka*s), escorted by 30 fighters, ran smack into a swarm of about 50 American Grumman 6F6 Hellcat fighters, some fifty or sixty miles before reaching their intended targets. The Hellcats shot down 15 of the 18 Bettys and decimated their fighter escort. The surviving 3 Bettys ducked into a covering cloud bank and were never seen again.

Overall, the Thunder Gods of the Cherry Blossom squadrons fared poorly—only three actually exploded on target. But no one could fault their extraordinary courage and kamikaze spirit.

The Kamikaze Spirit

To understand the attitudes and beliefs of the kamikazes—their willingness to die and acceptance of death—it is essential to recognize that they looked upon their life-ending assignments as merely another aspect of their duty. Commander Tadashi Nakajima, kamikaze operations and training officer, wrote after the war that many expressed their attitude like this:

> When we became soldiers, we offered our lives to the Emperor. When we sortie, it is with the firm conviction that we will fulfill this offer and help defeat the enemy. We would be remiss to think otherwise. Therefore, "special attack" is just a name. The tactic, while unusual in form, is just another way of performing our military obligation.[71]

This theme generally prevailed in their attitudes, Nakajima adds, and seldom did he witness displays of theatrics or hysterics. It was simply a case of doing one's duty, and

A Kamikaze Farewell

Kamikaze pilots rarely flew to their deaths while intoxicated, but they shared a cup of sake (Japanese rice wine) together before their final flight. In *Kamikaze,* surviving suicide pilot Yasuo Kuwahara describes (with Gordon T. Allred) a kamikaze farewell:

> Around the shaved skull of each Kamikaze was bound a small flag [usually a hachimaki, or headband], the crimson rising sun over his forehead. These departures were never conducted in a perfunctory manner. There was much ceremony, much show, toasts and valiant speeches—most of which I had already learned by rote. . . .
>
> "And so valiant comrades, smile as you go. . . . There is a place prepared for you in the esteemed presence of your ancestors . . . guardian warriors . . . samurai of the skies. . . ."
>
> And at last it was time to sing the battle song:
>
> "The Airman's color is the color of the cherry blossom.
>
> Look, the cherry blossoms fall on the hills of Yoshino.
>
> If we are born proud sons of the Yamato race,

> Let us die fighting in the skies."
>
> Then the final toast. The *sake* glasses were raised and the cry surged: *Tennoheika Banzai!* (Long live the Emperor).

Kamikaze pilots engage in a farewell ceremony in which they share a glass of sake before boarding their planes for the final mission.

most pilots approached their final assignment as they would any other.

An early American reaction to the kamikazes pictured them as crazed fanatics, hopped up on either dope or alcohol or both in order to carry out their missions. Not true. Traditionally, kamikaze pilots often shared a cup of sake (Japanese rice wine) before their final flights, but they rarely found courage in dope or drink. Nor was it necessary in most cases to compel pilots to plunge to a premature death in battle. Bernard Millot, aviation journalist and historian, observes:

> Unlike most other countries going through a difficult period in a war, Japan never had to resort to the well-known means of propaganda and coercion to reinvigorate the fighting spirit of her armed forces. The principle of combat without survival, of sublime effort—in short, the kamikaze spirit—was a permanent norm that went into effect whenever circumstances required it.[72]

On November 5, 1944, the Japanese Army Air Service's First Special Attack Unit—known as the *Banda Sakura* (Ten Thousand Cherry Blossoms)—joined their naval kamikaze brethren in action in the Philippines. Senior Japanese air officer Lieutenant General Kyoji Tomonaga addressed five special attackers before their departure, in words epitomizing the kamikaze spirit:

> When men decide to die like you they can move the heart of the Emperor. And I can assure you that the death of every one of you will move the Emperor. It will do more—it will even change the history of the world.
>
> I know what you feel now as you put the sorrows and joys of life behind you because the Emperor's fortunes are failing. Do not worry about what happens when you die and what you leave behind you—for you will become gods. Soon I hope to have the privilege of joining you in glorious death.[73]

The five army pilots then took to the air out of Clark Field and headed south toward Leyte Gulf. About eighty miles from the field, they met a group of U.S. carrier bombers on their way to assault Japanese bases. All five *Banda Sakura* pilots targeted an American bomber and rammed it. Circumstances would require similar actions for two more months of savage fighting for the Philippines.

☆ Chapter 6 ☆

The Rising Wind

"By combining the suicide dive with the lessons gained in past actions and a careful analysis of our defensive system, particularly our use of radar, the Japanese have developed the latest and most threatening problem that has yet confronted the U.S. Navy."

—Air Intelligence Group, Division of Navy Intelligence
(quoted in Denis Warner, Peggy Warner, with Sadao Seno,
The Sacred Warriors)

Although circumstances continued to worsen for the Japanese in the Philippines, a steady flow of reinforcements from Formosa enabled the Combined Land-based Air Force, augmented by army body-crashing units, to intensify kamikaze operations. While the U.S. Navy paused in late November to regroup its forces, land-based air force planes were to have provided air support for the army. But monsoon rains had rendered Leyte airfields inoperational, thus the task reverted to the carrier-based planes of Vice Admiral Mark A. Mitscher's Task Force 38.

Vice Admiral Mark A. Mitscher (pictured) and his Task Force 38 would soon feel the fury of the rising divine wind as reinforcements joined the kamikaze units.

The kamikazes lashed out at TF 38 (part of Admiral William F. Halsey's Third Fleet) with renewed fury.

Of Faith and Failure

On November 25, 1944, several roving kamikaze units lit upon TF 38 at twilight off the coast of Leyte. Thirteen suicide planes with a nine-plane escort slashed into Mitscher's carriers in two waves. In an assault that lasted about twenty-five minutes, the kamikazes smashed into three fleet carriers (CVs)—the *Essex*, the *Intrepid*, and the *Hancock*—and two light carriers (CVLs)—the *Cabot* and the *Independence*. Three kamikazes struck the hard-luck *Intrepid*, a ship with a history of ill fortune. "For God's sake," shouted the carrier's gunnery officer when the third suicide plane struck her, "are we the only ship in the ocean?"[74]

As a fleet carrier burns on the horizon, damage-control parties battle the inferno aboard one of the light carriers struck by kamikazes on November 25, 1944.

The attack seriously damaged the fleet carriers and left all five carriers burning, but alert damage-control parties soon brought the fires under control. All five vessels sustained heavy casualties but survived. Halsey withdrew them from action and sent them for repairs to Ulithi atoll, a forward navy base about twelve hundred miles to the southeast. "We got our tail feathers burned . . . and, frankly, we had to get out in a hurry,"[75] commented Rear Admiral Robert B. Carney, Halsey's chief of staff.

While the ships underwent repairs at Ulithi, Commander John S. (Jimmy) Thach, a fighter-pilot hero of the Battle of Midway, worked out a plan to better protect the task force carriers. "I developed a system of combined offense and defense in depth," he explained later. Offensively, his plan called for a "three strike system to keep fighter patrols over enemy airfields almost continuously."[76] In daylight, one strike would circle over an enemy airfield, strafing or bombing as needed to disrupt ground activities, while a second strike was being readied aboard a carrier. Meanwhile, a third strike would be en route to or from the enemy airfield. After dark, fighters and torpedo bombers would attack Japanese airstrips at odd intervals, strafing and bombing sporadically to minimize takeoffs.

Defensively, Combat Air Patrols were to range as far as sixty miles from a carrier task force. Thach called his system a "big blue blanket."[77] (Navy planes were painted blue on their upper surfaces and a lighter sky color on their undersides.) The navy adopted it as the standard tactic for countering kamikazes.

The suicide pilots struck several more times on November 26, notably an attack that evening against troop transports in Leyte Gulf by twenty-five planes—the largest group of kamikazes yet assembled. According to battle records, however, the kamikazes mounted one of their most devastating assaults of the Philippine campaign the next day. Both army and navy pilots took part in the attack. Attacking from several directions shortly before 1100 on November

Vapor trails stream from the propeller of a Hellcat as it waits for the takeoff signal. Soon the camouflaged fighter would join the "big blue blanket" on Combat Air Patrol.

27, about thirty Japanese planes broke through a ring of defending U.S. fighters and tore into twenty ships of Rear Admiral Thomas C. Kinkaid's Seventh Fleet.

One kamikaze plunged into the bow of the light cruiser *St. Louis*, setting off a flash of fire. Four more attackers swooped down on a second light cruiser, the *Montpelier*. Not one ship escaped attack—including the battleship *Colorado*—as, reportedly, other kamikazes joined the attack. Raymond Lamont-Brown writes:

> In all eight aircraft attacked *Montpelier*, five scoring direct hits. The ship was able to retain formation, but the crew saw for the first time the carnage of a suicide hit; pilots' shattered body fragments were everywhere—a tongue, scalp, brains, kneecaps and other bones hanging among the wreckage were hosed into the sea.[78]

His wing ripped off by antiaircraft fire, a suicide pilot presses home his attack. Such valor and sacrifice would not turn back the American fleet.

"Nip[ponese] planes seemed all over the sky," reports Commander Arthur M. Purdy, captain of the U.S. destroyer *Abner Reed*, during a similar earlier attack. Purdy gives this account of the destructive force of a kamikaze:

> Our barrage of fire ripped off [the wings of the kamikaze] but he still kept coming. He apparently dropped his bomb about a hundred yards from the ship and it went down the after stack, exploding in our steaming boiler. The plane itself practically swept away the whole midship section and within a matter of seconds the entire after deck house was one tremendous fire fanned by the wind. Seven or eight minutes later a tremendous explosion, undoubtedly a five-inch magazine going up, shook us. The ship immediately

sagged by the stern and ten minutes later sank.[79]

Suicide pilots twice attacked ships of the U.S. amphibious force near Leyte on November 28 and closed out November action the following day, attacking the Task Group 77.2 formation steaming on a northerly course in the Leyte Gulf on November 29. The kamikazes landed solid hits on the battleship *Maryland* and on the destroyers *Saufley* and *Aulick*. All three warships suffered great damage and took substantial casualties but stayed afloat, reflecting credit on the capacity of American shipbuilders to crank out ships at an incredible rate without compromising strength or fighting ability.

The kamikazes continued to reward Admiral Onishi's faith in his creation—at a great cost in pilots and planes—but what the admiral refused to either see or accept

An Unsettling Event

In an extract from "Target of a Suicide Bomber"—which forms a part of *Typewriter Battalion: Dramatic Frontline Dispatches from World War II*, edited by Jack Stenbuck—Chicago *Sun* foreign service correspondent John Graham Dowling describes a kamikaze attack:

ABOARD U.S. DESTROYER IN MINDANAO SEA, Dec. 13, 1944. . . . Suddenly, from the bridge came a sharp order and the talker near you repeated: "Action port!"

All eyes swung apprehensively to the left and then, with a soul-shaking sound, your 5-inch guns opened up. . . .

There was the Jap, a twin-engined bomber high and distant off the port beam, moving between the black bursts of our 5-inchers. . . .

The situation was perfectly understood. The Jap was hit and burning and was already as good as dead, and he had chosen to put his bombs on your ship before he died. As for your people, they faced the problem of blasting him out of the air before he could finish his run. . . .

[The kamikaze flew through a wall of 5-inch and 40- and 20- mm gunfire and drew to within 75 yards of the destroyer, then wavered.] You were aware of the steel from your ship's guns simply eating into the cabin of the oncoming Jap, simply putting so much fire into it that even a mouse in it could not stay alive.

In a moment of time, engulfed in a steel well of shocking sound and unbearable light, the Jap's wing tipped lower and touched the water, and in a flaming smash it was over as a pillar of orange fire and black smoke rose upon the water just 40 yards from your bridge.

The Jap plane had vanished and your ship's fire had stopped, and your ears were ringing like the bells of St. Patrick's on Easter, and your heart was like a piece of meat in the ice-box.

Dimly, through the cotton in your ears, came the vague cheers of the gun crews as their eyes went back to the skies to look for the next one and you, the observer, went down to the captain's cabin to the captain's washroom and threw up your lunch.

was that their sacrifices had not deterred the American advance.

Kamikaze Action Shifts to Luzon

Elements of the U.S. Seventy-seventh Infantry Division landed at Ormoc Bay, Leyte, on December 7, squeezing the Japanese between two American forces. The Japanese continued fighting doggedly for several more weeks, but the outcome was assured. Kamikazes struck hard at Rear Admiral Arthur D. Struble's Amphibious Group 9, however, sinking two U.S. destroyers, the *Mahan* and the *Reid,* and badly damaging but not disabling a third, the *Caldwell.*

Air force fighters, outnumbered and overwhelmed, were unable to fend off the streaking kamikazes. "Jap planes were falling like rockets all over the place," recalls one officer. "Falling isn't really correct because they were coming in under full power to pile into our ships."[80] As frightening and damaging as the suicide attacks were to the targeted enemies, the kamikazes failed to halt the American advance.

On December 15, some twenty-seven thousand more of General MacArthur's troops stormed ashore without opposition at Mindoro, an island stepping-stone between Leyte and the all-important main island of Luzon. One veteran combat

Troops of the Seventy-seventh Infantry Division come ashore at Ormoc Bay on December 7, 1944, the third anniversary of the Japanese attack on Pearl Harbor.

engineer viewed the unopposed landings with disdain, commenting that the "operation was just a maneuver for shore party units."[81]

Those aboard the light cruiser *Nashville,* flagship of the U.S. invasion fleet, could hardly agree with the engineer's assessment. Struck by a kamikaze dive-bomber two days earlier, the cruiser lost more than 130 killed and 190 wounded. Those killed included Brigadier General William C. Dunkel, commander of the landing force.

Suicide attackers subsequently sank two LSTs (landing ship, tank) and damaged several other vessels on December 15, and sank two more LSTs and damaged several more on December 21. Kamikaze attacks sent five more ships to the bottom and damaged a number of others on the final two days of December.

In December, anticipating an American invasion of Luzon in early January, Admiral Onishi moved his headquarters from Manila to Clark Field. By mid-December, only about forty Japanese aircraft remained operational in the Philippines, to which were added thirteen suicide Zeros flown in from Formosa. The kamikazes, determined to maximize the destructive force of their few remaining aircraft, ended their attacks on Mindoro at the start of 1945 and shifted to a new target—a huge Allied invasion fleet shaping course toward Lingayen Gulf on Luzon.

The Wind Also Rises

On January 2, Vice Admiral Jesse B. Oldendorf, aboard his flagship *California* (one of the battleships risen from the mud of Pearl Harbor), led Task Group 77.2 Bombardment and Fire Support Group out of

The Pennsylvania, *one of the repaired veterans of the Pearl Harbor attack, leads a column of Vice Admiral Oldendorf's task group.*

Leyte Gulf and set course for Luzon. Oldendorf's armada consisted of 164 ships—6 old battleships, 12 escort carriers, 10 destroyers, 63 minesweepers, and 73 auxiliary vessels. The kamikazes struck TG 77.2 two days later, on January 4.

One plane, a single-engine Judy bomber, slipped through Allied defenses undetected and smashed into the *Ommaney Bay*, which erupted in flames and soon shook with violent internal explosions when the flames reached the CVE's magazines. Her captain ordered her abandoned and later sunk by the destroyer *Burns* to prevent her smoking remains from attracting more attackers.

Kamikazes returned the next day to score hits on two heavy cruisers, the *Louisville* and the HMAS *Australia* (an Australian ship); two escort carriers, the *Manila Bay* and the *Savo Island;* and a destroyer, the HMAS *Arunta*. Vice Admiral C. R. Brown later summed up the emotions of those who bore the brunt of the suicide attacks:

We watched each plunging kamikaze with the detached horror of one witnessing a terrible spectacle rather than as the intended victim. We forgot self for the moment as we groped hopelessly for the thoughts of the man up there. And dominating it all was a strange admixture of respect and pity—respect for any person who offers the supreme sacrifice to the things he stands for, and pity for the utter frustration which was epitomized by the suicidal act. For whatever the gesture meant to that central actor out there in space, and however painful might be the consequences to ourselves, no one of us questioned the outcome of the war now rushing to its conclusion.[82]

Onishi's death divers struck even harder the next day, scoring two hits on the battleship *New Mexico* and the destroyer minesweeper *Long;* single hits on

Shipmates

On January 9, 1945, a kamikaze Zero struck the U.S. light cruiser *Columbia* (CL-56) off Luzon. In *Kamikaze Nightmare*, author Ron Burt presents his brother's recollection of the event. At 0745 that morning, Pete Harold Burt, an aviation ordnance mate aboard the cruiser, heard hostile gunfire:

I tell my marine shipmates [in their gunsight tub], Alvin and Jack, that something is getting too close. . . . Machine gun bullets are ricocheting off the forward superstructure.

Here is this Jap Zero coming at us. The Zero is only about 50 feet above the surface of the water. I observe all of this in just a matter of a split second before impact. The pilot and I look at each other. . . . I shout "DUCK!" The noise of the explosion drowns out my warning.

Fire and smoke erupt with a gigantic roar as the Zero crashes into the main superstructure hitting the main [gun] battery director. Flaming debris and smoke rise five hundred feet into the air. . . .

The Zero crashes twenty-five feet from where I stand. The explosion carries me thirty feet into a life line. My body burns with hot shrapnel covering me from head to foot. My left arm is practically blown to pieces. The muscle rips out from the shoulder to my elbow exposing broken bones. Hanging halfway over the life line, I lay stunned as numbness comes over my entire body. . . .

Nothing is left [of the shattered gun tub] but a tangled mass of jagged metal. Smoke and the odor of burning paint and human flesh stings my nostrils. In ankle deep blood, only broken bones and raw flesh remain of my two marine shipmates.

the battleship *California*, the cruisers *Columbia, Louisville,* and *Australia*, the destroyers *Walke, Allen M. Sumner,* and *O'Brien,* the destroyer transport *Brooks;* and near misses on numerous other warships.

Kamikaze attacks continued off Luzon until the Japanese ran out of planes around mid-January. By then, the kamikazes had sunk 24 ships, severely damaged 67 others, killed almost 800 sailors, and wounded about 1,400 more, many of them badly burned or maimed. These totals represented only a small sampling of things to come.

Official Japanese records show that 424 aircraft of varying types took part in suicide missions in the Philippines, in which some five hundred airmen perished. Japanese aviation became virtually extinct in the islands, and the staff and remaining pilots of the First and Second Air Fleets left Luzon for Formosa (now Taiwan) to organize new kamikaze units.

Manila fell to MacArthur's forces on March 4. Two weeks later, the dynamic gen-

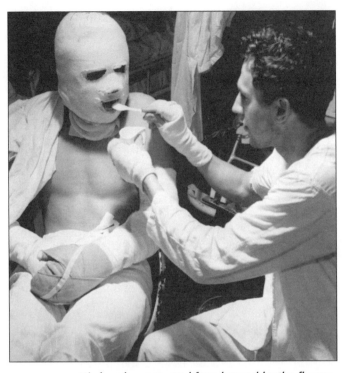

His hands, arms, and face burned by the flames of a kamikaze strike, an American sailor is fed by a navy medic.

eral returned to Corregidor and issued this order: "Hoist the colors and let no enemy ever haul them down."[83] In the meantime, the Divine Wind had risen again to wreak further havoc off Formosa and a tiny ashen island called Iwo Jima.

Chapter 7

Increased Action off Formosa and Iwo Jima

"It has never been difficult to become so exalted in the heat of combat as to defy the worst odds, to fight when necessary, to attack when outnumbered. All these things comprise the life of a man dedicated as a warrior. . . . But how does one quietly and objectively decide in a few hours to go out and kill oneself?"

—Saburo Sakai, one of Japan's greatest war aces, after receiving orders to crash-dive into an American carrier off Iwo Jima (in Saburo Sakai, with Martin Caidin, *Samurai!*)

On January 10, 1945, the day after some sixty-eight thousand Americans started swarming ashore on Lingayen's beaches to initiate the largest U.S. land campaign of the Pacific War, Admiral Onishi and his staff flew out of Luzon to Tainan, Formosa. (American B-29 long-range bombers were by then mounting frequent bombing raids on Formosa and the Japanese home islands, but evacuation between raids was still possible.) Several days later, Admiral Fukudome fled to Singapore by flying boat. Most of the air-support personnel of the Combined Land-based Air Force re-

mained in the Philippines to serve as defensive ground troops.

In Formosa, Onishi, as if possessed by a death wish, set about reorganizing his First Air Fleet kamikazes for one last grasp at glory. A new special attack unit was activated on January 18, composed of veteran pilots who had already volunteered for suicide missions and fledgling pilots from Formosan training centers, and was divided into five elements. The new unit was titled the Niitaka unit, after the highest mountain in Formosa.

At the christening ceremony, Admiral Onishi delivered a short address similar to his first speech at Mabalacat. "Even if we are defeated, the noble spirit of this kamikaze corps will keep our homeland

Message from a Dead Pilot

Surviving kamikaze pilot Yasuo Kuwahara witnessed the awesome spectacle of a fellow kamikaze turning back shortly after takeoff on his last flight and plunging his aircraft into his own hangar. In *Kamikaze*, Kuwahara (with Gordon T. Allred) describes a scene "which helped to sap our waning morale":

He had plunged into the main hangar, and the flames were climbing. Within seconds the hangar was a holocaust. . . .

Twenty of the best remaining fighters [on Formosa] were exploding like popcorn—a beautiful fireworks display. Thousands of gallons of stored fuel went next. Nothing could be salvaged.

Later, a letter was found among the dead man's possessions. Apparently written that morning, it contained some terse statements regarding Japan's plight and the futility of war, and the conclusion read: "My fellow comrades, by the time you read these words I will be dead. Do not judge me in anger. What is done, is done for a good reason. Perhaps our leaders, and men everywhere, will come to realize the stupidity of war some day, and perhaps through my own feeble and miserable efforts some of you may live. Japan's surrender is imminent, and by the time you read these words there will be twenty fewer planes for men to waste their lives in." Two of his friends tore up that letter and devoured it, but its message soon rumored about the base.

from ruin," he said. "Without this spirit, ruin would certainly follow defeat."[84] (His words suggest that he had already conceded defeat at that point.)

On January 21, Onishi received word of an American task force (TF 38) approaching Formosa from two hundred miles east-southeast of the island. He quickly launched three attack sections made up of Zekes and Judys: No. 1 Section (from Shinko), two Judys and two Zekes, with two Zeke escorts; No. 2 Section (from Taitung), two Judys and two Zekes, with three Zeke escorts; and No. 3 Section (from Taibu), two Judys, with two Zeke escorts.

American Hellcats shot down several of the attackers before they reached TF 38. Four kamikazes made it through to execute their dives. Two crashed into the fleet carrier *Ticonderoga*, one struck the light carrier *Langley*, and a fourth missed hitting the *Ticonderoga* and smashed into the nearby destroyer *Maddox*. Extreme damage forced both the *Ticonderoga* and the *Maddox* to withdraw to the forward naval base at Ulithi. The *Ticonderoga* never returned to action. Six of the seven Zeke escorts made it back to Tainan.

Meanwhile, American planes from TF 38 carriers were raining bombs on various Formosan targets, sinking ten ships at anchor (freighters and tankers), damaging several others, and destroying about sixty Japanese planes on the ground. On balance, the Niitaka unit could little claim tit for tat in the day's violent exchange.

Inspirational Action off Iwo Jima

By February 1945, B-29 bombing raids had become commonplace over the Japanese home islands, demoralizing civilians and workers and disrupting Japan's war production. The Boeing bomber flew so high and fast and was so well built and fortified—it was called the Superfortress—that conventional fighter tactics proved all but ineffective against it. Out of frustration and a sincere desire to lessen the devastating effects of the bombings on their country, family, and friends, Japanese fighter pilots often tried to ram the B-29s as the only effective means of dealing with them.

The Japanese high command neither condemned nor encouraged these individual ramming actions, likely withholding its approval to preserve as many aircraft as possible for the impending defense of

Japan. They feared that Iwo Jima or Okinawa—or even the southernmost Japanese island of Kyushu—might be the next American objective but in any case felt powerless to deter the Americans' next move.

When the Fifth Air Fleet, formed on February 11, promoted a preemptive strike against the U.S. fleet at anchor at Ulithi, the idea drew spirited support. The high command envisioned it as a potential second Pearl Harbor. They appointed fifty-four-year-old Vice Admiral Matome Ugaki, the Fifth Air Fleet's new commander, to organize a massive suicide attack against Ulithi, called the *TAN* (Sincere Loyalty) Operation.

Meanwhile, a U.S. bombing attack in the Tokyo-Yokohama area prompted pilots of the Third Air Fleet in Kyushu to clamor for a suicide attack squad of their own. On February 19, Vice Admiral Kimpei Teraoka, their commander in chief, obliged them and christened a new special attack force out of his 601st Air Group. Aircraft for the new force, called *Mitate* (Sacred Shield) Unit No. 2, consisted of a mix of thirty-two fighters, bombers, and torpedo bombers, mostly Zekes and Judys, split into five groups.

B-29 Superfortresses were almost immune to conventional fighter tactics, and many Japanese pilots resorted to crashing into the bombers.

83

Also on February 19, American forces crammed ashore on the black-sand beaches of Iwo Jima. The *TAN* Operation, in which the *Mitate* unit was slated to participate, was put on temporary hold. Two days later *Mitate* Unit No. 2 was committed to more pressing action against elements of Admiral Raymond A. Spruance's TF 58 off Iwo Jima. Late that day all five *Mitate* groups suddenly appeared out of a thick cloud cover and began their dives on the surprised task force before antiaircraft gunners could react effectively.

Three kamikazes struck the fleet carrier *Saratoga;* two more speared into the escort carrier *Bismarck Sea,* sinking her; and a sixth rammed into the escort carrier *Lunga Point.* *Mitate* pilots also scored hits on the cargo ship *Keokuk* and two LSTs. Several escorts,

The flight deck of the Saratoga *burns after three kamikazes slammed into it on February 19, 1945. Five other ships were sunk or damaged in the attack.*

apparently swept up in the action, tried unsuccessfully to crash into enemy vessels, but their failure did not negate the overall success of *Mitate* Unit No. 2's mission.

Their success did not go unnoticed by the defenders on Iwo Jima. The kamikaze action "greatly inspired" Lieutenant General Tadamichi Kuribayashi, commander of the Iwo Jima garrison. In a speech to his troops, he said, "No man must die until he has killed at least ten Americans. We will harass the enemy with guerrilla actions until the last of us has perished. *Tenno Banzai!* (Long live the Emperor!)"[85]

The Battle of Iwo Jima lasted for several bloody weeks. Of the more than 21,000 Japanese defenders, only 1,083 surrendered. General Kuribayashi committed ritual suicide on March 27.

The kamikaze spirit inspired the Japanese troops defending Iwo Jima. Only a few chose to surrender to U.S. marines.

The *TAN* Operation

While the fighting still raged on Iwo Jima and an Allied ring of steel began to close on Japan itself, the Imperial Japanese Navy decided to reorganize and redistribute its air fleets for maximum effectiveness. Thus, the IJN high command formed the Tenth Air Fleet on March 1. The reorganization and redeployment looked like this: the First Air Fleet, 300 planes based on Formosa; the Third, 800 planes scattered about different airfields in the eastern half of Japan; the Fifth, 600 planes covering the western half of the country; and the Tenth, 400 aircraft spread across the home islands.

On March 7, a Japanese reconnaissance plane reported that the U.S. fleet, after having completed its support operations off Iwo Jima, had returned to its base at Ulithi. The Fifth Air Fleet put together a suicide attack group within twenty-four hours and the long-awaited *TAN* Operation was finally set in motion.

Pilots of the newly formed *Azusa* (after the wood used to make samurai bows) unit gathered on March 10. With *hachimakis* (head scarves) in place, they toasted each other with sake, a present from the emperor. Fifth Air Fleet commander Ugaki cautioned them to return should success in their mission appear impossible. "There is no need to go rushing to death,"[86] he told them just before takeoff.

The *Azusa* unit consisted of nine reconnaissance planes for guidance and a main strike force of twenty-four Frances twin-engine land-based bombers, each carrying a 1,760-pound bomb. En route to their target, they were recalled because of an erroneous report that the American fleet had disappeared from Ulithi. They tried again the next morning.

The attack group assembled over Cape Sata, at the southern tip of Kyushu, at 0930 and set a southeasterly course for Ulithi. Thirteen Frances bombers developed engine trouble and had to land at emergency fields. Two ditched in the ocean. Rough weather forced the rest of the group to detour around rain squalls, extending the distance that was already pressing the maximum range of the twin-engine bombers. The guide planes sighted Yap Island, about thirty minutes from Ulithi, at 1830 and returned to base.

The remaining eleven Frances bombers reached Ulithi at 1905 and commenced diving on the brightly lit U.S. base. (Because of Ulithi's remote location, the Americans had discounted any possibility of an enemy attack.) One suicide bomber struck the fleet carrier *Randolph*, causing minimal damage, and that was all. The attack fell far short of Japanese expectations of a second Pearl Harbor. "It was evident that this attack had failed,"[87] observed Captain Rikihei Inoguchi, in what some might consider something of an understatement. Meanwhile, the Americans were stepping up their attacks on the Japanese home islands.

Invasion Timetable

On the night of March 9–10, 1945, more than three hundred B-29s pummeled the citizens of Tokyo, dumping thousands of incendiaries on the Japanese capital and turning one-quarter of the city into a wind-whipped firestorm. "I watched people, adults and children, dashing madly about like rats," recounts one survivor. "The flames raced after them like living things, striking them down."[88] As many as 100,000 people succumbed in the holocaust, which destroyed some 267,000 dwellings.

The attack on Tokyo set the pattern for subsequent B-29 raids targeting Nagoya, Kobe, Osaka, Yokohama, and Kawasaki—cities representing the heart of Japan's industrial strength. By firebombing them into virtual extinction, American strategists hoped to cauterize the kamikaze spirit from the hearts and minds of the Japanese people—and thus save countless American lives by negating the need to invade Japan.

Nor did military targets in Japan escape attention. Even as the last kamikaze plunged to his death at Ulithi, Admiral Marc A. Mitscher's Task Force 58—comprising ten heavy and six light carriers split into four task groups—was steaming into position for a large-scale attack on Japan

More than three hundred B-29s attacked Tokyo during the night of March 9–10. Firestorms from the assault consumed one-quarter of the city.

proper. From March 18 to 21, preparatory to the American invasion of Okinawa, carrier planes from TF 58 (now part of Admiral Spruance's Fifth Fleet) lashed out at airfields in Kyushu and enemy shipping at Kobe and Kure in the Inland Sea.

On March 18, Japanese reconnaissance planes reported the approach of TF 58. Kamikazes, escorts, and conventional bombers of Admiral Ugaki's Fifth Air Fleet—some fifty in all—rose out of Kyushu airfields to intercept the American

warships. They probably passed TF 58's incoming carrier planes unknowingly, while en route to their targets at sea and what is generally considered the opening action of the Okinawa campaign.

When Ugaki's planes arrived over target, the escorts engaged TF 58's Hellcat defenders, while the kamikazes and conventional bombers commenced their dives. As usual, the kamikazes targeted the American carriers. Within minutes the fleet carriers *Enterprise* and *Franklin* were struck and damaged by conventional bombers but not severely enough to warrant their withdrawal from action. In this attack, the kamikazes managed to damage only the destroyer *Halsey Powell* and the submarine *Devilfish*.

The next day TF 58 aircraft launched a second attack on the Kyushu airfields and assaulted fleet targets at Kobe and Kure. It was the first time carrier planes had struck targets in Honshu and the Inland Sea. This time, kamikaze and conventional bombers of the Tenth Air Fleet struck at TF 58 in several groups. One group of twenty Judy conventional dive-bombers managed to slip through violent antiaircraft fire and damaged three fleet carriers: the *Wasp*, seriously; the *Essex*; and, for the second time in two days, the *Franklin*.

Two 550-pound bombs struck the *Franklin*, setting ablaze planes being fueled and armed on her flight deck and rocking the carrier with two enormous explosions fed by her own munitions and gasoline stores. No one expected the *Franklin* to survive the huge blasts. Admiral Mitscher signaled permission to abandon ship from his

Mauled by two 550-pound bombs, the Franklin *remained afloat despite flames on the flight deck and explosions deep within the ship.*

Seen from the cruiser Pittsburgh, *the* Franklin *is towed out of the impact zone. The* Franklin *later made the voyage to the Brooklyn Navy Yard under her own power.*

flagship carrier *Bunker Hill*. Captain Leslie H. Gehres, the *Franklin*'s skipper, declined. "Hell, we're still afloat!"[89] he responded indignantly. And miraculously she stayed afloat.

A superhuman effort by the *Franklin*'s crew brought her raging fires under control using the latest fire-control equipment and methods. The cruiser *Pittsburgh* then towed the badly listing *Franklin* out of the impact zone. Her casualties totaled 1,100, including 830 dead. Later, she steamed some twelve thousand miles under her own power to her home berth in Brooklyn Navy Yard. By then, she looked "almost presentable."[90] Thanks to the efforts of her valiant captain and crew, she endured to become the most shattered carrier on either side to survive the war.

During March 18–19, Admiral Ugaki hurled 193 aircraft at TF 58, including 69 kamikazes. His losses totaled 163 destroyed, or 83 percent, while 50 more sustained damage on the ground. Ugaki's brief air action against TF 58 culminated with the inauspicious debut of the new *Ohka* piloted bomb on March 21.

After the first *Ohka* mission, Captain Motoharu Okamura, the officer primarily responsible for the Thunder Gods Corps, blamed Admiral Ugaki for the mission's abject failure:

> The attack was a total failure because there were not enough covering planes protecting the Bettys, and because there was no element of surprise. The whole process of using Thunder Gods has to be reexamined.[91]

It would seem an apt criticism.

Sources vary widely as to the results of TF 58's attacks on Kyushu airfields and fleet units at Kure and Kobe. (It is common for sources to vary where numbers and dates are involved—often to the extreme.) Figures supplied by Lieutenant R. L. Wehrmeister, USN, offer a likely account of what happened:

> Five hundred twenty-eight enemy planes were destroyed, sixteen enemy surface craft were damaged, and scores of hangars, factories, and warehouses were destroyed or damaged at a total cost of 116 American planes. This attack [March 18–21] resulted in the Japanese being unable to mount any strong air attack against our forces for almost a week after the initial landings on Okinawa.[92]

The American invasion timetable held to schedule, and the stage was set for the last great battle of the Pacific War.

Chapter 8

Zenith at Okinawa

"Fear plagues me. I ask myself: 'Will I suffer at the moment of the explosion?' I answer at once: 'Ugh! It's not worth thinking about. The pain will last only a flash, perhaps a tenth of a second. . . .'"

—Flying Officer Ryuji Nagatsuka's thoughts while en route to Okinawa on an aborted suicide mission (*I Was a Kamikaze*)

The Divine Wind blew strongest and longest during the struggle for Okinawa, the last battle of World War II. Okinawa is the largest island of a group centered in the 600-mile-long chain of Ryukyu Islands. It lies 350 miles southwest of Japan. Heavily fortified and staunchly defended, it represented the last stepping-stone to Japan in Admiral Nimitz's island-hopping campaign in the Pacific.

Lieutenant General Mitsuru Ushijima, commander of some 135,000 Japanese defenders, swore to defend the island to the death of his last man. He felt confident that

his troops could hold back the invaders long enough for the kamikazes and suicide boats (*Shinyos*) to annihilate the American

General Mitsuru Ushijima felt his troops could block the American assault on Okinawa until kamikazes and suicide boats could destroy the invasion fleet offshore.

91

The Turning Point

While the kamikazes were launching *Kikusui* No. 1 on April 6, Vice Admiral Sejichi Ito's Second Fleet got underway in the Inland Sea and headed for Okinawa. Ito's surface force consisted of the Imperial Japanese Navy's last ten warships—the monster battleship *Yamato*, the light cruiser *Yahagi*, and eight destroyers. They sailed without air cover. The mighty *Yamato* carried only enough fuel for a one-way voyage. Before departing Tokuyama Oil Depot at 1524 that afternoon, Vice Admiral Ito issued this message to his fleet (as quoted by Russell Spurr in *A Glorious Way to Die*):

> This operation will be the turning point of the war. The future of the empire rests on our efforts. Every man will do his utmost for the glory of the Imperial Navy and of Japan.

That evening, the U.S. submarines *Threadfin* and *Hackleback,* while patrolling the Bungo Strait exit from the Inland Sea, reported several unidentified Japanese warships steaming in a southerly direction. When Admiral Mitscher received their report, he immediately dispatched twelve of his fast carriers to intercept the enemy warships.

A scout from the U.S. carrier *Essex* sighted the Japanese warships at 1000 the next morning. Wave after wave of American planes commenced attacking the *Yamato* at 1235. After nearly four hours of constant pummeling by dive-bombers and torpedo planes, the *Yamato* slid under at 1623, with 2,488 officers and men. The *Yahagi* suffered a similar end, as did four destroyers. The other four destroyers, though damaged, escaped and fled home.

On that day, the Japanese lost 3,655 sailors against American losses of some 15 aircraft and 84 pilots and seamen. The Imperial Japanese Navy had fought its last surface battle.

The battleship Yamato *narrowly avoids a bomb dropped by an American plane off Okinawa. Navy bombers and torpedo planes would soon sink her.*

fleet offshore. At the very least, he hoped to weaken the U.S. fleet and amphibious corps enough to force the Americans to delay or cancel any attempt to invade Japan itself.

Ushijima's chief of staff, Major General Isamu Cho, also exuded confidence. While addressing the commanders of the Thirty-second Army, he shared his vision of the kamikazes. "The brave ruddy-faced warriors with the white silken scarves tied about their heads, at peace in their favorite planes, dash out spiritedly to the attack," he said. "The skies are brightening."[93]

However, the light came not from the brilliance of exploding kamikazes but from the glow of Japan's setting sun.

Heavenly Operation

Convinced that kamikaze attacks represented the only effective means of countering the powerful Allied forces at Okinawa, the Japanese high command ordered that they be exploited to the fullest extent. To that end, an Okinawa defense plan called *Ten-Go* (Heavenly Operation) was developed at the start of 1945.

Briefly, the plan called for a joint army-navy all-out air attack on the Allied invasion fleet, using more than four thousand aircraft, both suicide and conventional. Several hundred suicide speedboats operating from scattered bases in Okinawa and the Kerama Islands to the southwest would support the aerial action. Finally, Japan's few remaining warships, including the mighty superbattleship *Yamato*, would dash from the Inland Sea to join the fray and battle to the death.

The high command appointed Vice Admiral Matome Ugaki as overall commander of the combined operation. The major thrust of the kamikaze operations was to originate from airfields in Kyushu, with Vice Admiral Takijiro Onishi's Formosa-based special attack unit contributing little to the defense of Okinawa. Onishi himself was reassigned to serve as vice chief of the Naval General Staff in Tokyo, where he finished out the war behind a desk.

On February 6, a joint army-navy agreement outlined the plan's key provisions:

In general Japanese air strength will be conserved until an enemy landing is underway or within the defense sphere. . . . Primary emphasis will be laid on the speedy activation, training and mass deployment of the Special Attack Forces (*kamikaze*). . . . The main target of Army aircraft will be enemy transports, and of Navy aircraft carrier attack forces.[94]

The battle for Okinawa, which saw the kamikazes soar to the zenith of their combat effectiveness, commenced on April 1, 1945—Easter Sunday. It began quietly, with Japanese defenders offering such little resistance that marines called L-Day (Landing Day) "Love Day." Japanese resistance remained light for almost a week, prompting marine veteran and historian Robert Leckie to remark, "Love Day turned into Honeymoon Week."[95] But the honeymoon ended abruptly on April 6.

Kikusui No. 1

The kamikazes operated only sporadically during the first days of fighting (largely because of TF 58's successful raids on kamikaze airfields in Japan two weeks earlier), but they struck with massive force on the sixth day. Combining forces for the first time, the Japanese army and navy amassed 700 aircraft—355 of them kamikazes, the rest fighters and bombers, some carrying piloted *Ohka* bombs—and launched the largest kamikaze assault of the war.

In Japan, the chrysanthemum is perhaps the most cherished of all flowers. They were often woven into wreaths and dropped at sea by mourning pilots onto the watery graves of fallen comrades. In observance of this honored tradition, Admiral Ugaki decided to assign the name of *Kikusui*, or "Floating Chrysanthemums," to the scheduled *Ten-Go* aerial attacks. Thus, the attack of April 6–7, the first of a total of ten, is often enumerated as *Kikusui* No. 1. This first joint aerial assault filled the Okinawan skies with swarms of suicide planes attacking around the clock for two days.

During those forty-eight hours, Hellcat and Corsair fighters from Admiral Mitscher's TF 58 carriers shot down 250 enemy planes before they even reached the radar picket screen. (Radar-equipped picket ships, usually destroyers, were positioned as far as sixty miles away from the carriers, in the direction of an expected attack, to provide early warning. For this reason, destroyers absorbed the brunt of kamikaze attacks off Okinawa.) Another 55 attackers fell inbound to the main fleet and 171 more during their final runs. "In just a few minutes," notes Walter J. Boyne, aviation historian and archivist, "476 chrysanthemums floated no more."[96]

Nonetheless, 180 kamikazes got through to their targets to strike hard at the invasion fleet. "Two destroyers, one high-speed minesweeper, and one LST went to the bottom," recounts navy lieutenant R. L. Wehrmeister, "while eleven destroyers, one high-speed minesweeper, three escort vessels, three minesweepers, and the aircraft carrier *Hancock* were damaged."[97]

The Americans lost 466 killed and 568 wounded, as well as suffering a hefty jolt to morale over being targeted by human bombs, during the two days of *Kikusui* No. 1. And there were nine more general attacks still to come.

Corsair fighter planes lie aboard a US carrier. Their wings are folded to save space.

April Showers

The massed *Kikusui* attacks resumed on April 12 and continued until June 22, but none reached the magnitude of the first attack of April 6–7. And with each successive attack, the number of kamikazes involved slowly diminished—185 on April 12–13 (*Kikusui* No. 2), 165 on April 15–16 (No. 3), and so on.

The Thunder Gods entered the action during *Kikusui* No. 2, when Lieutenant Saburo Dohi piloted his *Ohka* rocket-bomb into the starboard side of the destroyer *Stanley*. Another *Ohka* struck the water about two thousand yards away. Later that day a third *Ohka* smashed into the middle

The aircraft carrier Hancock *burns after being hit by elements of* Kikusui *No. 1.*

of the destroyer *Mannert L. Abele* to record the first *baka* bomb kill. The *Abele* sank five minutes later.

Throughout the *Kikusui* attacks, the radar picket ships—mostly destroyers—took it on the chin. The kamikazes believed that they would gain clear access to the larger ships closer to Okinawa by first destroying the U.S. early warning system. After weathering a two-day suicide attack, the innovative crew of one picket ship rigged a large sign with an arrow pointing to the main fleet and the words: "To Jap Pilot—This Way to Task Force 58." [98]

One hundred sixty-five deadly flowers of *Kikusui* No. 3 shed further petals of destruction on the American fleet during April 15–16. In one memorable sequence, kamikazes attacked the destroyer *Laffey* twenty-two times from every angle in a seventy-nine-minute period and scored five hits, but the tough little ship survived.

Lieutenant Commander Frank A. Manson, communications officer aboard the *Laffey*, later described the aftermath of those seventy-nine minutes on the picket line:

> It all looked peaceful, except for a few grim reminders: bloated bodies of suicide pilots floated by, along with bits of their planes, drifting like leaves with the tide—constant reminders, if such were needed, of the deadly seriousness of Japanese purpose." [99]

A kamikaze struck and sank the destroyer *Pringle* at another picket station, and seven other vessels absorbed crash-dive hits before the third two-day attack ended. The suicidal winds slacked off after *Kikusui* No. 3, and picket-line sailors welcomed a twelve-day respite of relative calm. Even so, spasmodic kamikaze attacks continued to rain terror on the American navy.

On April 23, Central Pacific Commander Admiral Chester W. Nimitz, deeply concerned with the mounting naval casualties and ship losses, flew from Guam to Okinawa to confer with Tenth Army Commander Lieutenant General Simon Bolivar Buckner. "I'm losing a ship and a half a day," he told General Buckner. "So if this line [of U.S. forces on Okinawa] isn't moving within five days, we'll get someone here to move it so we can all get out from under these damn air attacks." [100] (An amphibious assault on the enemy rear by the Second Marine Division loomed as a viable alternative to a purely frontal assault.) The kamikazes had begun to impact U.S. strategy at the highest level.

The lethal winds picked up again during April 27–28, as 115 suiciders of *Kikusui* No. 4 showered death and destruction on the invasion fleet and TF 58, sinking the destroyer *Haggard* and the *Canada Victory,* a converted merchant ship loaded with ammunition. Seven other ships took hits to close out April's deadly showers.

May Flowers

Floating Chrysanthemums continued to blossom and fall during four more massed attacks in May. *Kikusui* No. 5 struck on May 4–5, sinking the destroyers *Little, Luce,* and *Morrison* and two LSMs (landing ship, medium), while damaging ten other vessels. The destroyer *Aaron Ward*, hit multiple times, the destroyer escort *England*, and the escort carrier *Sangamon* were damaged so severely that they were later scrapped.

Aboard the *Sangamon*, twenty-four-year-old Lieutenant Malcolm Herbert McGann was dazed by the first of two kamikazes that struck the carrier. A long time later he lauded the Japanese pilot. "He was a better man than I was—the guy who went through our flight deck," he said. "I couldn't have done it."[101]

May 10–11 saw four kamikazes inaugurate *Kikusui* No. 6 by crashing into the destroyer *Evans*. A fifth kamikaze and an *Ohka* smashed into the destroyer *Hugh W. Hadley*. Both ships were towed to a safe anchorage only to be scrapped. The fleet carrier *Bunker Hill*, Admiral Mitscher's flagship, took direct hits from a Zeke and a Judy and was rocked by explosions, becoming the second most badly damaged ship to

survive the war (next to the *Franklin*). Admiral Mitscher transferred his flag to the carrier *Enterprise*.

The seventh *Kikusui* assault erupted during May 23–25 in a series of uncommonly violent attacks in which some 160 suiciders took part. After a one-day break in the action, the kamikazes followed with *Kikusui* No. 8, committing a hundred more death dives during May 27–28. These two operations combined to sink four destroyers and an LSM, while critically damaging fourteen others. Among the latter, six destroyers had

Last Words

The world will never know the final views on life of thousands of kamikazes standing at the edge of eternity. This brief sampling of last messages, extracted from naval historian Roger Pineau's "Spirit of the Divine Wind," reflects a range of emotion that was typical among the doomed pilots.

Ensign Susumu Kaijitsu effused love of family and an eagerness to fulfill his mission:

> We are hopeful of leading our divine Japan to victory. . . . Words cannot express my gratitude to the loving parents who reared and tended me to manhood. . . . Think kindly of me and consider it my good fortune to have done something praiseworthy. . . . I pray for your well being.

Ensign Teruo Yamaguchi expressed misgivings:

> I was selected unexpectedly and am leaving for Okinawa today. . . . Life in the service has not been filled with sweet memories. . . . I can see only that it gives one a chance to die for his country. . . . It leaves a bad taste in my mouth when I think of the deceits played on

our innocent citizens by some of our wily politicians. I am willing to take orders . . . because I believe in the polity of Japan.

Cadet Jun Nomoto wrote with quiet confidence:

> I am confident of my ability . . . [and] will do my utmost. My friends and I must part company, but there is no remorse. Every man is doomed to go his own way in time. . . . We have had the most intensive training. Now, at last our chance to sortie has arrived. . . . It is my firm belief that tomorrow will be successful.

Ensign Heiichi Okabe wrote bitterly in his diary:

> Death and I are waiting. . . . I shall die watching the pathetic struggle of our nation. I am a human being—with hope to be neither scoundrel nor saint, fool nor hero—just a human being. . . .

> We die in battle without complaint. I wonder if those not in uniform would do the same. Only then can Japan have any prospect of winning.

Men scramble to contain the fires caused by two kamikaze hits aboard Bunker Hill *(above). One of the attacking planes tore clean through the ship's flight deck (right).*

to be scrapped. But by the end of May, the flowers of *Yamato* were wilting fast.

"Neither Saints nor Devils"

In spite of the terror and destruction spread across April and May by the Floating Chrysanthemums, Japan was unable to match the awesome power or deter the relentless advance of the Americans. The longer the drain on Japanese pilots and planes continued with no sign of accomplishing Japan's purpose, the greater the demoralizing effect became on the kamikazes.

At first, most pilots who stepped forward to fly officially sanctioned death missions for the sake of family, country, and the emperor were in the truest sense volunteers. They responded to the requests of their commanding officers without hesitation and seemingly without qualms. (However, when considering what it means to volunteer, it should be remembered that an officer's request is traditionally taken as a command by subordinates in virtually all military services around the world. In other words, an officer's request is tantamount to a direct order.) As the kamikaze attacks wore on, however, and the sacrifices of their predecessors failed to make any apparent difference in altering the course of the war, attitudes began changing among young pilots slated for suicide missions. The thought of dying without making a difference held little appeal for many of them.

"Early in the Okinawa campaign pilots could go to their deaths with some hope that their country might realize some benefit from their sacrifice," writes Rear Admiral Toshiyuki Yokoi, chief of staff to the Fifth Air Fleet during the Okinawa campaign. "But toward the last, the doomed pilots had good reason for doubting the validity of the cause in which they were told to die." Pilots in training started displaying a growing sense of futility and resentment when ordered into action. Adds Yokoi:

When it came time for their takeoff, the pilots' attitudes ranged from the despair of sheep headed for slaughter to open expressions of contempt for their superior officers. There were frequent and obvious cases of pilots returning from their sorties claiming that they could not locate any enemy ships, and one pilot even strafed his commanding officer's quarters as he took off.[102]

Irrespective of whatever they might have felt, most kamikaze pilots accepted their lot with stoic calm and flew off to their deaths with implacable obedience—but not all. Perhaps naval historian Roger Pineau states their case best:

Gunners of the carrier Hornet *score a bull's-eye on a kamikaze aiming at their ship.*

Devotion to duty was not an invariable rule at this critical stage of the war. The special attackers were neither saints nor devils. They were human beings, with all the emotions and feelings, faults and virtues, strengths and weaknesses of other human beings.[103]

Chief among their virtues was uncommon courage.

The Final Days

Uncommon courage was commonplace among those youthful kamikazes, who continued to do all that was asked of them during the last two scheduled attacks in June. Some fifty pilots flew to their deaths with marginal results in *Kikusui* No. 9, during June 4–7, turning two destroyers into scrappage and damaging an LCI (landing craft, infantry). Another forty-five kamikazes accomplished little more in the last *Kikusui* attack (No. 10), during June 21–22, sinking an LSM and damaging two destroyers, an LSM, and an LST.

Pilots of *Kikusui* No. 10 flew to their deaths unaware that their last missions coincided with the end of organized Japanese resistance on Okinawa. At 0300 on June 22, Lieutenant General Mitsuru Ushijima slit open his belly in traditional *seppuku* style. His adjutant decapitated him to complete the ritualistic suicide. The kamikazes, individually and in small groups, continued to harass the U.S. Navy off Okinawa—particularly ships of the picket line—until the war ended.

Final figures on the destruction wrought by the kamikazes varies enormously from source to source (even among purported official U.S. sources). Figures compiled by naval historian Clark G. Reynolds and the editors of Time-Life Books are offered here as a reasonable summation:

A total of 1,465 Japanese Army and Navy aircraft flown by kamikaze pilots had been dispatched to Okinawa between April and June. They had sunk 26 American ships and damaged 164 others, including Mitscher's flagship, the *Bunker Hill*, which was knocked out of the War.[104]

The kamikazes reached their zenith in the Okinawa campaign—the heights of incredible bravery—but they failed to turn the war to Japan's advantage. In the end, the dark waters of the Pacific claimed the youthful flower of Japanese manhood, and the Floating Chrysanthemums and Cherry Blossoms floated no more. Perhaps, if immortality stems from pure courage and sincerity of purpose, their flower will bloom again in some honored afterworld reserved for only the bravest of the brave.

If in one's heart
He follows the path of sincerity,
Though he does not pray,
Will not the gods protect him?[105]

And will not his spirit reside eternally on call in the Yasukuni Shrine, waiting patiently to serve again?

The Way of the Samurai

Like cherry blossoms
 In the spring
 Let us fall
 Clean and radiant.[106]

The blossoms fell in flights that failed to alter the outcome of World War II. Six weeks after the fall of Okinawa, U.S. airmen dropped the first atomic bomb on Hiroshima on August 6, 1945, and a second on Nagasaki three days later. Two Japanese cities and some 135,000 people vanished instantly in two sudden, blistering flashes of heat and light. Thousands more perished later.

In one of the great ironies of the war, the resolute, self-sacrificing tactics of the Japanese, so exemplified by the kamikazes, may have contributed greatly to America's willingness to employ atomic force. The alternative, as American strategists viewed it, would mean invading a nation of kamikazes at the cost of several million more American and Japanese lives. In any event, the two world-shattering blasts brought a quick end to the war.

On August 15, in a taped radio broadcast, Emperor Hirohito informed his subjects of Japan's acceptance of Allied

Nagasaki, August 1945. Some 135,000 people died instantly here and in Hiroshima, but millions would have perished had the U.S. invaded Japan.

demands for an unconditional surrender. He said, in part:

> The enemy has begun to employ a new and inhuman bomb, the power of which to do damage is indeed incalculable, taking a toll of many innocent lives. To continue the war under these conditions would not only lead to the annihilation of Our Nation, but to the destruction of human civilization as well. . . . It is according to the dictate of time and fate that We have resolved to pave the way for a grand peace for all generations to come by enduring the unendurable and tolerating the intolerable.[107]

The nation mourned en masse following Hirohito's announcement, but not everyone looked forward to "enduring the unendurable," or to anything else having to do with surrender. The kamikaze spirit flared anew—briefly but brightly—in the hearts of a few die-hard dissenters.

Onishi's End

Vice Admiral Takijiro Onishi, the father of the kamikazes, dined at home with friends on the evening of August 15. After dinner he retired to his second-floor study and wrote a letter. He then disemboweled himself and sliced his own throat with a jagged

Japanese prisoners on the island of Guam hang their heads after hearing of Japan's surrender.

blade. He had been ordered to turn the tide of war at whatever the cost and he had failed.

The aging warrior had spent his last days wandering about official Tokyo, bending the ears of his colleagues, trying to drum up support in high places for a fight to the last man. Hirohito's surrender message at noon left him empty and twice defeated. His aide found Onishi later that night still conscious, but he refused both medical aid and the traditional coup de grâce—beheading. Instead, he elected to suffer the pain of a lingering twelve-hour death. Afterward, his letter was found in which he wrote:

> I wish to express my deep appreciation to the souls of the brave special attackers. They fought and died valiantly with faith in our ultimate victory. In death I wish to atone for my part in the failure to achieve that victory and I apologize to the souls of these dead fliers and their bereaved families.[108]

Clearly, the creator of the kamikaze corps felt deep respect for his fledglings and bore total responsibility for their deaths. In life, he wore an expressionless face that veiled his emotions—the mask of command. In death, he left behind words to strip away the samurai's facade and reveal his true sensitivity.

Last Attacks

Onishi's unwavering successor, Vice Admiral Matome Ugaki—schooled in the samurai tradition of preferring an honorable death to a shameful surrender—also dissented on August 15. The night before, upon hearing rumors of the emperor's pending capitulation, he issued the following order: "Oita Detachment of 701st Air Group will attack the enemy fleet at Okinawa with three dive bombers. The attack will be led by the commanding admiral."[109]

His subordinates tried to dissuade him, sometimes tearfully, but to no avail. When Ugaki arrived at the airstrip—after the emperor's address had confirmed the surrender rumor—instead of three planes he found eleven, with engines roaring and twenty-two airmen standing ready for departure. Lieutenant Tatsuo Nagatsuru, the unit commander, explains: "Who could stand to see the sortie limited to only three planes when Admiral Ugaki himself is going to lead the attack. Every plane of my command will join."[110]

Four planes turned back due to engine trouble, but Ugaki and the others continued on toward Okinawa. The admiral's last radio message to his base stated:

> I alone am to blame for our failure to defend the homeland and destroy the arrogant enemy. . . . I am going to make an attack at Okinawa where my men have fallen like cherry blossoms. There I will crash and destroy the conceited enemy in the true spirit of Bushido, with firm conviction and faith in the eternity of Imperial Japan.

The last words of the message were "Long live His Imperial Majesty the Emperor!"[111] Shortly thereafter, another message reported that Admiral Ugaki was about to dive. Similar reports soon followed from the six others. None were heard from again. No American ship reported a kamikaze on August 15.

It remains a mystery as to why the admiral apparently failed to realize that a successful attack on any American ship might have ignited a renewal of hostilities.

Despite the questionable wisdom inherent in his last act, Vice Admiral Matome Ugaki died as he had lived—in the noble way of the samurai.

A group of *Shinyo*s attacked a British aircraft carrier squadron entering Hong Kong harbor on August 30, 1945, and were strafed, bombed, and sunk by British aircraft or beached themselves in the last suicide attack of the war. Japan formally surrendered to the Allies on September 2, 1945.

Efficacy and Morality

More than a half century after the first kamikaze plunged into the crucible of

Japanese envoys sign the documents of surrender aboard the battleship Missouri *in Tokyo Bay on September 2, 1945. General MacArthur stands at right.*

modern warfare, military analysts, historians, and scholars continue to debate the efficacy and morality of suicide as a weapon. As regards the effectiveness of the kamikazes, the Okinawa campaign demonstrated that the kamikazes compiled a 20 percent hit rate against Allied vessels, with 25 percent of those hit either sunk or rendered inoperable.

On the other hand, critics point out that such operations cannot hope for success in situations where aircraft and trained pilots are limited. Moreover, according to aviation historian Walter J. Boyne, the kamikaze concept is otherwise flawed. Boyne explains:

> The Japanese, who lost more than 500 aircraft in the [Philippine] attacks, never grasped the hard physical fact that most of their planes, even at the end of their fatal plunge, didn't have the mass required to cause fatal damage. A bomb dropped by a speeding dive-bomber reaches its terminal velocity, multiplying its mass upon impact. The kamikaze aircraft, even those that dove into their targets, were unable to reach the speed required to do ship-sinking damage.[112]

Thus physics adds to the effectiveness arguments that continue to rage. It should also be noted that secondary and tertiary explosions of fuel and ordnance contributed to many of the ship sinkings attributed to the kamikazes.

Seki's Song

As quoted in *The Sacred Warriors: Japan's Suicide Legions,* Lieutenant Yukio Seki, lead pilot of the first successful kamikaze mission, left this haiku for the pilot trainees who had been under his command:

Fall my pupils,
My cherry blossoms,
Just as I will fall
In the service of our land.

In moral terms, Western minds may never come to accept the premise of officially sanctioned and directed suicide. Indeed, even the parents of kamikazes loudly renounced the suicide missions after the war. Many Japanese derided the missions as having "violated the basic tenets of humanity." Others scorned them for inscribing the Japanese in history's annals as "savages in a barbaric country."[113]

One of the more outspoken military critics of kamikaze tactics was Rear Admiral Toshiyuki Yokoi, chief of staff to the Fifth Air Fleet. In a critique of the Okinawa campaign after the war, Yokoi writes: "The whole concept of suicide attacks to annihilate enemy task forces was more than unreasonable, it was sheer lunacy." Yokoi contends that a misinterpretation of the true spirit of Bushido permitted human life to be treated lightly and concludes:

> Japan's suicide air operations mark the Pacific War with two scars that will remain forever in the annals of battle:

one, of shame at the mistaken way of command; the other, one of valor at the self-sacrificing spirit of young men who died for their beloved country.[114]

The debate remains open-ended. Perhaps no conclusions should be drawn before carefully contemplating the insightful perceptions of kamikaze staff officer Captain Rikihei Inoguchi. "The arguments and criticisms of the rest of the world as to the morality of the kamikaze tactics are in a way academic," he writes. "They seem relatively unimportant compared to the convictions, the feelings of the kamikaze pilots themselves."[115]

"The way of the samurai is found in death,"[116] writes Tsunetomo Yamamoto, an

At the Yasukuni Shrine in 1995, former kamikazes Fujio Hayashi, Morimasa Yunokawa, and Hideo Suzuki (left to right) stand in front of a model of an Ohka.

eighteenth-century samurai. By war's end, reportedly 2,940 kamikazes had discovered the way of the samurai. Honor the brave and judge them not unkindly.

★ Notes ★

Introduction: One-Way Flights to Eternity

1. Quoted in Hanson W. Baldwin, "The Greatest Sea Fight: Leyte Gulf," in *Reader's Digest Illustrated Story of World War II*. Pleasantville, NY: Reader's Digest Association, 1969, p. 473.

2. Quoted in Baldwin, "The Greatest Sea Fight: Leyte Gulf," p. 473.

3. Quoted in Edward Jablonski, *Airwar*, vol. II. Garden City, NY: Doubleday, 1971, p. 177.

4. Quoted in Denis Warner and Peggy Warner, with Sadao Seno, *The Sacred Warriors: Japan's Suicide Legions*. New York: Van Nostrand Reinhold Company, 1982, p. 69.

5. Quoted in Warner and Warner, *The Sacred Warriors,* p. 70.

6. Stephen Turnbull, *Samurai Warfare*. London: Arms and Armour Press, 1996, p. 44.

7. Stephen Turnbull, *Samurai: The Warrior Tradition*. London: Arms and Armour Press, 1996, p. 39.

8. Quoted in Ronald H. Spector, *Eagle Against the Sun: The American War with Japan*. New York: The Free Press, 1985, p. 410.

9. Mitsuo Fuchida and Masatake Oku- miya, *Midway: The Battle That Doomed Japan: The Japanese Navy's Story*. Annapolis, MD: Naval Institute Press, 1955, p. 262.

10. Ryuji Nagatsuka, *I Was a Kamikaze*. Translated by Nina Rootes. New York: Macmillan, 1972, p. 156.

Chapter 1: Japan and the Sources of Suicide

11. Boye De Mente, "Introduction," in Hatsuho Naito, *Thunder Gods: The Kamikaze Pilots Tell Their Story*. New York: Kodansha International, 1989, p. 20.

12. Harry Cook, *Samurai: The Story of a Warrior Tradition*. New York: Sterling, 1993, p. 8.

13. Yuri Tanaka, *Hidden Horrors: Japanese War Crimes in World War II*. New York: Westview Press, 1996, pp. 204–205.

14. Tanaka, *Hidden Horrors*, pp. 205–206.

15. James R. Ware, "Introduction," in Confucius, *The Sayings of Confucius*. Translated by James R. Ware. New York: New American Library, 1955, p. 19.

16. *Compton's Interactive Encyclopedia*, version 3.00, copyright © 1994, 1995 Compton's New Media, Inc. All rights reserved.

17. John Toland, *The Rising Sun: The Decline and Fall of the Japanese Empire, 1936–1945,* vol. 1. New York: Random House, 1970, pp. 72n, 73.
18. Tanaka, *Hidden Horrors,* p. 207.
19. Cook, *Samurai,* p. 6.
20. Quoted in Warner and Warner, *The Sacred Warriors,* p. 40.
21. Quoted in Raymond Lamont-Brown, *Kamikaze: Japan's Suicide Samurai.* London: Arms and Armour Press, 1997, p. 18.
22. Warner and Warner, *The Sacred Warriors,* pp. 39–40.
23. Quoted in Naito, *Thunder Gods,* p. 209.
24. Quoted in Nagatsuka, *I Was a Kamikaze,* p. 166.
25. Quoted in Tanaka, *Hidden Horrors,* p. 203.

Chapter 2: "A Fitting Place to Die"
26. Spector, *Eagle Against the Sun,* p. 487.
27. Quoted in Peter Maas, "The Battle of the Philippine Sea," in *Reader's Digest Illustrated Story of World War II,* p. 456.
28. Nagatsuka, *I Was a Kamikaze,* p. 47.
29. Quoted in Jablonski, *Airwar,* p. 136.
30. Quoted in Nathan Miller, *War at Sea: A Naval History of World War II.* New York: Scribner, 1995, p. 450.
31. Quoted in Miller, *War at Sea,* p. 449.
32. Quoted in Thomas J. Cutler, *The Battle of Leyte Gulf: 23–26 October 1944.* New York: HarperCollins Publishers, 1994, p. 68.
33. Quoted in Jablonski, *Airwar,* pp. 137–38.
34. Toland, *The Rising Sun,* p. 664.
35. Quoted in Cutler, *The Battle of Leyte Gulf,* p. 66.
36. Quoted in David Bergamini, *Japan's Imperial Conspiracy.* New York: Pocket Books, 1972, p. 1,079.
37. Quoted in Cutler, *The Battle of Leyte Gulf,* p. 67.

Chapter 3: Genesis in the Philippines
38. Quoted in Stephen E. Ambrose and C. L. Sulzberger, *American Heritage New History of World War II.* New York: Viking, 1997, p. 143.
39. Quoted in Ambrose and Sulzberger, *American Heritage New History of World War II,* p. 527.
40. Quoted in Rikihei Inoguchi, Tadashi Nakajima, and Roger Pineau, *The Divine Wind: Japan's Kamikaze Force in World War II.* New York: Ballantine Books, 1972, pp. 5–7.
41. Quoted in Bernard Millot, *Divine Thunder: The Life and Death of the Kamikazes.* New York: Pinnacle Books, 1970, p. 49.
42. Quoted in Inoguchi, Nakajima, and Pineau, *The Divine Wind,* p. 9.
43. Quoted in Warner and Warner, *The Sacred Warriors,* p. 87n1.
44. Quoted in Rikihei Inoguchi and Tadashi Nakajima, translated and condensed by Masataka Chihaya and Roger Pineau, "The Kamikaze Attack Corps," *U.S. Naval Institute Proceedings,* September 1953, p. 936.
45. Quoted in Millot, *Divine Thunder,* p. 50.

46. Quoted in Warner and Warner, *The Sacred Warriors*, p. 88.
47. Quoted in A. J. Barker, *Suicide Weapon*. Illustrated History of the Violent Century series, Weapons Book no. 22, editor-in-chief Barry Pitt. New York: Ballantine Books, 1971, p. 74.
48. Quoted in Nagatsuka, *I Was a Kamikaze*, p. 144.
49. Nagatsuka, *I Was a Kamikaze*, p. 144.
50. Inoguchi, Nakajima, and Pineau, *The Divine Wind*, p. 11.
51. Quoted in Inoguchi, Nakajima, and Pineau, *The Divine Wind*, pp. 11–12.
52. Quoted in Millot, *Divine Thunder*, pp. 52–53.
53. Quoted in Lamont-Brown, *Kamikaze*, pp. 40–41.
54. Quoted in Cutler, *The Battle of Leyte Gulf*, p. 270.

Chapter 4: Expanding Kamikaze Operations

55. Quoted in Inoguchi, Nakajima, and Pineau, *The Divine Wind*, pp. 60–61.
56. Quoted in Inoguchi, Nakajima, and Pineau, *The Divine Wind*, p. 61.
57. Lamont-Brown, *Kamikaze*, p. 29.
58. Quoted in Warner and Warner, *The Sacred Warriors*, p. 59.
59. Quoted in Jablonski, *Airwar*, p. 175.
60. Quoted in Walter J. Boyne, *Clash of Wings: Air Power in World War II*. New York: Simon & Schuster, 1994, p. 262.
61. Quoted in Inoguchi and Nakajima, "The Kamikaze Attack Corps," p. 937.
62. Quoted in Bergamini, *Japan's Imperial Conspiracy*, p. 1,090.
63. Quoted in Jablonski, *Airwar*, p. 177.

Chapter 5: The Kamikazes

64. Roger Pineau, "Spirit of the Divine Wind," *U.S. Naval Institute Proceedings*, November 1958, p. 24.
65. Inoguchi, Nakajima, and Pineau, *The Divine Wind*, p. 81.
66. Quoted in Lamont-Brown, *Kamikaze*, p. 66.
67. Quoted in Warner and Warner, *The Sacred Warriors*, p. 121.
68. Nagatsuka, *I Was a Kamikaze*, p. 164.
69. Quoted in Nagatsuka, *I Was a Kamikaze*, p. 164.
70. Inoguchi, Nakajima, and Pineau, *The Divine Wind*, pp. 126–27.
71. Quoted in Inoguchi, Nakajima, and Pineau, *The Divine Wind*, p. 75.
72. Millot, *Divine Thunder*, p. 78.
73. Quoted in Lamont-Brown, *Kamikaze*, p. 71.

Chapter 6: The Rising Wind

74. Quoted in Clark G. Reynolds and the Editors of Time-Life Books, *The Carrier War*. Alexandria, VA: Time-Life Books, 1982, p. 157.
75. Quoted in Miller, *War at Sea*, p. 493.
76. Quoted in Reynolds, *The Carrier War*, p. 158.
77. Quoted in Reynolds, *The Carrier War*, p. 158.
78. Lamont-Brown, *Kamikaze*, p. 72.
79. Quoted in Miller, *War at Sea*, p. 492.
80. Quoted in Miller, *War at Sea*, p. 494.

81. Quoted in Spector, *Eagle Against the Sun*, p. 518.
82. Quoted in Jablonski, *Airwar*, p. 180.
83. Quoted in Ambrose and Sulzberger, *American Heritage New History of World War II*, p. 565.

Chapter 7: Increased Action off Formosa and Iwo Jima

84. Quoted in Inoguchi, Nakajima, and Pineau, *The Divine Wind*, pp. 110–11.
85. Quoted in Lamont-Brown, *Kamikaze*, p. 89.
86. Quoted in Warner and Warner, *The Sacred Warriors*, p. 177.
87. Quoted in Inoguchi, Nakajima, and Pineau, *The Divine Wind*, p. 119.
88. Quoted in Miller, *War at Sea*, p. 517.
89. Quoted in Reynolds, *The Carrier War*, p. 165.
90. Quoted in Robert Leckie, *Okinawa: The Last Battle of World War II*. New York: Viking, 1995, p. 47.
91. Quoted in Naito, *Thunder Gods*, p. 119.
92. R. L. Wehrmeister, "Divine Wind Over Okinawa," *U.S. Naval Institute Proceedings*, June 1957, p. 634.

Chapter 8: Zenith at Okinawa

93. Quoted in Jablonski, *Airwar*, p. 190.
94. Quoted in Leckie, *Okinawa*, p. 19.
95. Quoted in Jablonski, *Airwar*, p. 189.
96. Boyne, *Clash of Wings*, p. 273.
97. Wehrmeister, "Divine Wind Over Okinawa," p. 635.
98. Quoted in Miller, *War at Sea*, p. 526.

99. Frank A. Manson, "Seventy-Nine Minutes on the Picket Line," *U.S. Naval Institute Proceedings*, September 1949, p. 1,000.
100. Quoted in James H. Hallas, *Killing Ground on Okinawa: The Battle for Sugar Loaf Hill*. Westport, CT: Praeger, 1996, p. 10.
101. Quoted in Warner and Warner, *The Sacred Warriors*, p. 244.
102. Toshiyuki Yokoi, with Roger Pineau, "Kamikazes and the Okinawa Campaign," *U.S. Naval Institute Proceedings*, May 1954, pp. 510–11.
103. Quoted in Inoguchi, Nakajima, and Pineau, *The Divine Wind*, p. 1.
104. Reynolds, *The Carrier War*, p. 170.
105. Quoted in Tsunetomo Yamamoto, *Hagakure: The Book of the Samurai*. Translated by William Scott Wilson. New York: Avon Books, 1979, pp. 140-41.

Epilogue: The Way of the Samurai

106. Quoted in Roger Pineau, "Spirit of the Divine Wind," p. 28.
107. Quoted in Jablonski, *Airwar*, p. 213.
108. Quoted in Millot, *Divine Thunder*, p. 245.
109. Quoted in Inoguchi, Nakajima, and Pineau, *The Divine Wind*, p. 148.
110. Quoted in Roger Pineau, "Spirit of the Divine Wind," p. 29.
111. Quoted in Millot, *Divine Thunder*, p. 244.
112. Boyne, *Clash of Wings*, p. 267.
113. Quoted in Lamont-Brown, *Kamikaze*,

p. 173.

114. Yokoi, "Kamikazes and the Okinawa Campaign," pp. 510, 513.

115. Quoted in Inoguchi, Nakajima, and Pineau, *The Divine Wind,* p. 174.

116. Yamamoto, *Hagakure,* p. 17.

★ Glossary ★

ack-ack: Antiaircraft fire.

Amaterasu-o-Mikami: Japanese Sun Goddess from whom the Japanese people claim descent; sometimes called the Great Ancestress of Japan.

Asahi: Literally "Rising Sun"; name adopted by one of four units of the first kamikaze corps.

B-29: Boeing four-engine long-range bomber; the "Superfortress."

baka bomb: "Foolish" or "stupid" bomb; the Japanese piloted bomb called *Ohka* (Cherry Blossom).

Banda Sakura: Literally, "Ten Thousand Cherry Blossoms"; the Japanese Army Air Service's First Special Attack Unit.

banzai: Literally, "ten thousand years"; figuratively, when used in the context of a battle cry: "Hail to the Emperor! May he live for ten thousand years!"

banzai charge: A suicide charge.

Betty: Allied code name for the Mitsubishi G4M (Navy Type 97) torpedo bomber.

Buddhism: A complex system of beliefs originating in India, based on the teachings of the Buddha (or Enlightened One), Siddhārtha Gautama (563–483 B.C.).

bushi: Warrior; Japanese term used interchangeably with samurai.

Bushido or Bushido code: Literally, "The Way of the Warrior"; warrior code of conduct; originally practiced by the samurai of medieval Japan and perpetuated in modified (some say corrupted) form by Japanese armed forces in the twentieth century.

CAP: Combat Air Patrol.

CL: Light cruiser (USA).

Confucianism: A system of moral conduct founded in China by Confucius (551–479 B.C.).

CV: Fleet carrier (USA).

CVE: Escort carrier (USA).

CVL: Light carrier (USA).

daimyo: Local lord in feudal Japan.

DD: Destroyer (USA).

DE: Destroyer escort (USA).

Frances: Allied code name for the Yokosuka D4Y1 *Ginga* (Milky Way) land-based bomber.

geisha: In Japan, a skilled female entertainer and witty conversationalist.

Gunjin Chokuron: Japanese *Imperial Code of Military Conduct,* requiring absolute loyalty to the emperor.

gyokusai: Literally, "broken gem"; glorious self-annihilation; Japanese concept that prefers an honorable death in battle over the shame of surrender.

hakko ichiu: Literally, "the whole world under one roof," which really meant under the emperor; Japanese belief that they were predestined to rule the world because of their divine origins.

IJN: Imperial Japanese Navy.

"Imperial Rescript": A military code of conduct for Japanese soldiers and sailors issued by Emperor Meiji in 1882; an oath.

Izanagi: "The Male Who Invites"; Japanese mythical male god of creation; *see also* Izanami.

Izanami: "The Female Who Invites"; Japanese mythical female god of creation; *see also* Izanagi.

Jill: Allied code name for the Nakajima B6N *Tenzan* (Heavenly Mountain) carrier attack plane and torpedo bomber.

Jimmu Tenno: First emperor of Japan (ruled 660–585 B.C.); great-grandson of Amaterasu-o-Mikami, the Sun Goddess.

Jinrai Butai: Thunder Gods Special Attack Corps.

Judy: Allied code name for the Yokosuka D4Y *Suisei* (Comet) carrier-based bomber.

kami: Spirits; deities of natural forces.

kamikaze: Literally, "divine wind"; name assigned to Japanese suicide pilots or planes during World War II; *see also shimpu.*

LCI: Landing craft, infantry (USA).

LSM: Landing ship, medium (USA).

LST: Landing ship, tank (USA).

Mitate: Literally, "Sacred Shield"; name of five kamikaze groups.

Nirvana: In Buddhist and Hindu teaching, the state of perfect bliss attained when the soul is freed from all suffering and absorbed into the supreme spirit.

OCTAGON: Allied code name for the American invasion of the Philippines.

Ohka: Literally, "Cherry Blossom"; the Japanese name for the piloted bomb dubbed *baka* ("foolish" or "stupid") bomb by the Americans.

Peggy: Allied code name for the Mitsubishi Ki-67 *Hiryu* (Flying Dragon) standard bomber.

sake: Japanese rice wine.

samurai: Members of the warrior aristocracy of medieval Japan.

Senjin Kun: Ethics of Battle; official military code of ethics issued to the Japanese armed services in 1941 by then army minister General Hideki Tojo.

seppuku: Ritual suicide by disembowelment, more vulgarly known as *hara-kiri.*

Shikishima: Literally "Beautiful Island"; name adopted by one of four units of the first kamikaze corps.

shimpu: A variant interpretation of the Japanese characters for "kamikaze."

Shinto: The native religion of Japan; a loose system of beliefs and attitudes, closely aligned with the nation's system of values and the behavior of its people.

Sho: Japanese term for "victory" or "to conquer."

Sho Ichi Go: Operation Victory One; Japanese battle plan for the defense of the Philippines.

shogun: Chief military commander in feudal Japan.

shugo: State-appointed military governors in feudal Japan.

sortie: One flight by a single military plane.

strategy: The plan for an entire operation of a war or campaign.

tactics: The art of placing or maneuvering forces skillfully in a battle.

***TAN* Operation:** Code name for the unsuccessful kamikaze raid on the U.S. forward naval base at Ulithi atoll in the West Caroline Islands (*TAN* means "Sincere Loyalty").

Tenno Banzai!: Long live the Emperor!

Tokubetsu Kogekitai: Special Attack Corps or Squad.

Yamato: Literally, "Great Peace"; name adopted by one of four units of the first kamikaze corps; the old name for Japan and a general term for the Japanese people; and one of Japan's super battleships.

Yamato-damashii: The Japanese spirit.

Yamazakura: "Wild Cherry Blossom"; name adopted by one of four units of the first kamakaze corps.

Yasukuni-jinja: Yasukuni Shrine; literally, "Shrine of the Righteous Souls"; temple in Tokyo where the spirits of Japan's war dead dwell until called to fight again.

Zeke: Code name for Japanese fighter-bomber (Mitsubishi Zero-Sen); *see also* Zero.

Zero: Japanese fighter plane (Mitsubishi Zero-Sen); sometimes used as a fighter-bomber; *see also* Zeke.

★ Chronology of Events ★

1941

January 3: General Hideki Tojo (then army minister) issues new official code of ethics to every member of Japanese armed forces.

December 7: Imperial Japanese Navy attacks U.S. Pacific Fleet at Pearl Harbor.

1942

March 11: General MacArthur leaves Philippines, vowing to return.

1944

June 19–21: The Battle of the Philippine Sea (the Great Marianas Turkey Shoot).

June 25: Use of suicide as weapon sanctioned for first time by Emperor Hirohito.

July 9: Saipan falls to Admiral Nimitz's naval and amphibious forces.

August 2: Nimitz's forces capture Tinian.

August 10: Guam taken by Nimitz's forces.

September 15: Morotai falls to General MacArthur's forces.

October 1: The *Jinrai Butai* (Thunder Gods Special Attack Corps) formed; production of *Ohka* piloted bomb commences.

October 6: Soviets reveal American intentions to reclaim Philippines to Japanese ambassador in Moscow.

October 13: Peleliu falls to U.S. III Amphibious Corps.

October 15: Rear Admiral Masafumi Arima fails in attempt to crash his bomber into U.S. carrier *Franklin*, east of Luzon.

October 17: Japanese plans to defend Philippines (*Sho*-1) set in motion; Vice Admiral Takijiro Onishi assumes command of Japanese First Air Fleet.

October 19: First four units of Japanese Special Attack Corps formed at Mabalacat airfield on Luzon.

October 20: General MacArthur returns to Philippines.

October 25: First successful kamikaze attack carried out by *Shikishima* unit of Japanese Special Attack Corps against U.S. Navy task force in Philippines.

November 5: Japanese Army Air Service's First Special Attack Unit (*Banda Sakara*) rams U.S. carrier bombers in Philippines.

November 25–28: Kamikazes attack ships of TF 38 and Seventh Fleet off Leyte.

December 7: Elements of U.S. Seventy-seventh Infantry Division land at Ormoc Bay, Leyte.

December 13: U.S. light cruiser *Nashville* struck by kamikaze.

December 15: Twenty-seven thousand U.S. troops storm ashore at Mindoro; kamikazes sink two LSTs.

December 21: Kamikazes sink two LSTs and damage several more.

December 30–31: Kamikazes sink five U.S. ships and damage several others.

1945

January 2: Task Group 77.2 leaves Leyte Gulf for Luzon.

January 4 through mid-January: Kamikazes sink 24 ships, damage 67 others, kill almost 800 sailors, and wound about 1,400 more.

January 10: Sixty-eight thousand American troops land at Lingayen. Vice Admiral Onishi transfers kamikaze operations to Formosa (Taiwan).

January 18: Vice Admiral Onishi activates new kamikaze group called Niitaka unit.

January 21: Niitaka unit strikes TF 38 east-southeast of Formosa.

February: B-29 bombing raids become commonplace over Japan.

February 15: Japanese Fifth Air fleet formed.

February 19: American forces land at Iwo Jima. *Mitate* (Sacred Shield) Unit No. 2 formed from Third Air Fleet in Kyushu.

February 21: Five *Mitate* units attack TF 58 off Iwo Jima.

March 1: Japanese Tenth Air Fleet formed.

March 4: Manila falls to MacArthur's forces.

March 9–10: B-29s firebomb Tokyo.

March 11: Kamikaze *Azusa* unit raids U.S. forward naval base at Ulithi atoll.

March 18–21: Planes from TF 58 attack Kyushu and Honshu; kamikaze and conventional bombers attack TF 58 in opening action of Okinawa campaign.

March 21: First mission of *Jinrai Butai* (Thunder Gods Special Attack Corps) ends in total failure.

March 27: Lt. Gen. Tadamichi Kuribayashi, commander of Japanese troops on Iwo Jima, commits suicide.

April 6–7: Kikusui No. 1.

April 12–13: Kikusui No. 2.

April 15–17: Kikusui No. 3.

April 27–28: Kikusui No. 4.

May 3–4: Kikusui No. 5.

May 10–11: Kikusui No. 6.

May 23–25: Kikusui No. 7.

May 27–28: Kikusui No. 8.

June 3–7: Kikusui No. 9.

June 21–22: Kikusui No. 10; Japanese resistance on Okinawa ends.

August 6: U.S. airmen drop atomic bomb on Hiroshima.

August 9: U.S. airmen drop atomic bomb on Nagasaki.

August 15: Emperor Hirohito announces Japan's acceptance of Allied unconditional surrender terms; Vice Admiral Takijiro Onishi commits ritual suicide; Vice Admiral Matome Ugaki and several subordinates fly to their deaths in last aerial kamikaze attack of war.

August 30: A group of *Shinyo*s launch unsuccessful attack against British carrier squadron in Hong Kong harbor in last suicide attack of war.

September 2: Japan formally surrenders to Allies.

☆ For Further Reading ☆

Clay Blair Jr., *MacArthur.* Garden City, NY: Nelson Doubleday, 1977. A highly readable biography of a great American general, featuring a wide-ranging account of World War II in the Pacific.

———, *Silent Victory: The U.S. Submarine War Against Japan,* vol. II. Philadelphia: J. B. Lippincott, 1975. The definitive history of the submarine war against Japan, including coverage of kamikazes and *kaiten*s (manned torpedoes).

Anthony J. Bryant, *Samurai 1550–1600,* vol. 7 of the Osprey Warrior series. Edited by Lee Johnson. London: Osprey, 1996. A study of the samurai's skills with details of his battle equipment.

Harold L. Buell, *Dauntless Helldivers: A Dive-Bomber Pilot's Epic Story of the Carrier Battles.* New York: Bantam Doubleday Dell, 1991. A decorated navy pilot relates a personal account of dive-bomber action during World War II.

Martin Caidin, *Zero Fighter.* Illustrated History of World War II series, Weapons Book no. 9. New York: Ballantine Books, 1973. An exciting account of the agile, brilliant fighter plane that for a time ruled the Pacific skies in the Second World War.

Christopher Chant et al., *The Encyclopedia of Air Warfare.* New York: Thomas Y. Crowell, 1975. An excellent illustrated history of war in the air, with brief coverage of the kamikaze squadrons.

William Craig, *The Fall of Japan.* New York: Galahad Books, 1997. Craig depicts the final tumultuous weeks of World War II, when Japan had to choose between surrender and total annihilation.

Mitchell Dana, "Hold That Line . . . or Die," in *Reader's Digest Illustrated Story of World War II.* Pleasantville, NY: Reader's Digest Association, 1969. American invasion forces at Okinawa become the primary targets for Japanese suicide squadrons.

Jiro Horikoshi, *Eagles of Mitsubishi: The Story of the Zero Fighter.* Translated by Shojiro Shindo and Harold N. Wantiez. Seattle: University of Washington Press, 1981. The saga of the design, development, and performance of a great aircraft, many of which were used by the kamikazes in their final acts of desperation.

John W. Lambert, *Bombs, Torpedoes and Kamikazes.* North Branch, MN: Specialty Press, 1997. A pictorial history of the Imperial Japanese Navy's assault on the ships and aircraft of the U.S. Navy during World War II.

Edmund G. Love, "Banzai on Saipan," in *Reader's Digest Illustrated Story of World War II.* Pleasantville, NY: Reader's Digest Association, 1969. A recounting of the biggest suicide operation of World War II, a precursor to the suicidal kamikaze flights.

Paul W. Martin, "Kamikaze!" *U.S. Naval Institute Proceedings,* August 1946, pp. 1,054–57. Martin presents a brief overview of kamikaze activities during the last seven months of World War II.

I. E. McMillan, "The U.S.S. *Newcomb* (DD 586)—Victim of the Kamikazes," *U.S. Naval Institute Proceedings,* June 1948, pp. 682–89. A naval captain relates how one U.S. destroyer survived seven kamikaze attacks off Okinawa in the spring of 1945.

Miyamoto Musashi, *The Book of Five Rings.* Translated by Thomas Cleary. New York: Barnes & Noble Books, 1997. A new translation of the centuries-old Japanese classic on both the technical and spiritual elements of the confrontational skills of the martial arts.

Zenji Orita, with Joseph D. Harrington, *I-Boat Captain.* Canoga Park, CA: Major Books, 1978. A Japanese submarine captain writes about the undersea war in the Pacific, including stark coverage of Japanese suicide operations.

J. Davis Scott, "No Hiding Place—Off Okinawa," *U.S. Naval Institute Proceedings,* November 1957, pp. 1,208–13. A naval commander tells the strange story of a marine pilot caught up in intense kamikaze action off Okinawa in 1945.

Stephen Turnbull, *Samurai Warfare.* London: Arms and Armour Press, 1996. An examination of the reality of battlefield tactics, personalities, and practices of the samurai warrior.

Paul Varley, with Ivan Morris and Nobuko Morris, *The Samurai.* Pageant of History series. Edited by John Gross. London: Weidenfeld and Nicolson, 1970. The authors trace the evolution of Japan's warrior class from its tenth-century origins until modern times.

Hiromichi Yahara, *The Battle for Okinawa.* Translated by Roger Pineau and Masatochi Uehara. New York: John Wiley & Sons, 1995. A Japanese officer's eyewitness account of the last great campaign of World War II and the zenith of kamikaze operations.

★ Works Consulted ★

Stephen E. Ambrose and C. L. Sulzberger, *American Heritage New History of World War II*. New York: Viking, 1997. Ambrose's masterful updating, with new facts and two new chapters, of Sulzberger's standard reference work, first published in 1966.

Hanson W. Baldwin, "The Greatest Sea Fight: Leyte Gulf," in *Reader's Digest Illustrated Story of World War II*. Pleasantville, NY: Reader's Digest Association, 1969. A riveting account of the great sea battle that marked the debut of the kamikazes.

A. J. Barker, *Suicide Weapon*. Illustrated History of the Violent Century Series, Weapons Book no. 22. Editor-in-chief Barry Pitt. New York: Ballantine Books, 1971. The story of exceptionally brave men called upon to perform extraordinarily heroic deeds certain to result in their deaths.

David Bergamini, *Japan's Imperial Conspiracy*. New York: Pocket Books, 1972. An exhaustive and contentious study of Japan's role in World War II that indicts Emperor Hirohito as a war criminal.

Walter J. Boyne, *Clash of Wings: Air Power in World War II*. New York: Simon & Schuster, 1994. A popularly written, detailed survey of the role of airpower over land and sea in World War II.

Ron Burt, *Kamikaze Nightmare*. Corpus Christi: Alfie Publishing, 1995. The author describes the action and turmoil of American naval forces facing the horror of kamikaze attacks.

Compton's Interactive Encyclopedia, version 3.00, copyright © 1994, 1995, Compton's New Media. All rights reserved. The CD-ROM version of the venerable encyclopedia.

Confucius, *The Sayings of Confucius*. Translated by James R. Ware. New York: New American Library, 1955. Pointed stories and clever aphorisms attributed to the venerable Chinese philosopher.

Harry Cook, *Samurai: The Story of a Warrior Tradition*. New York: Sterling, 1993. A profusely illustrated work that pays tribute to the real and fascinating history of a unique warrior tradition.

Thomas J. Cutler, *The Battle of Leyte Gulf: 23–26 October 1944*. New York: HarperCollins Publishers, 1994. The author recounts the dramatic full story of the greatest naval battle in history.

C. B. Dear and M. R. D. Foot, eds., *The Oxford Companion to World War II*. New York: Oxford University Press, 1995. A one-volume masterwork on the greatest war in history, containing "more than 1,700 entries—ranging from brief identifications to in-depth articles on complex subjects," including Japan's kamikaze forces.

Ernest Dupuy and Trevor Dupuy, *The Encyclopedia of Military History: From 3500 B.C. to the Present.* Revised edition. Harper & Row, 1986. The definitive one-volume work on military history; includes concise account of kamikaze operations.

Trevor N. Dupuy, Curt Johnson, and David L. Bongard, *The Harper Encyclopedia of Military Biography.* New York: HarperCollins, 1992. An invaluable compilation and assessment of the three thousand most important worldwide military figures from earliest times to the present.

Robert B. Edgerton, *Warriors of the Rising Sun.* New York: W. W. Norton, 1997. A chronicle of the Japanese military's transformation from honorable "knights of bushido" into men who massacred thousands during the Pacific War.

Mitsuo Fuchida and Masatake Okumiya, *Midway: The Battle That Doomed Japan: The Japanese Navy's Story.* Annapolis, MD: Naval Institute Press, 1955. A valuable account of the battle as seen through the eyes of two Japanese naval officers who took part in the engagement.

The Hagoromo Society of Kamikaze Divine Thunderbolt Corps Survivors, *Born to Die: The Cherry Blossom Squadrons.* Edited by Andrew Adams. Los Angeles: Ohara Publications, 1973. Surviving Kamikaze Corps members tell how they resigned themselves to death to save the crumbling Japanese Empire.

James H. Hallas, *Killing Ground on Okinawa: The Battle for Sugar Loaf Hill.* Westport, CT: Praeger, 1996. A gritty account of one of the bloodiest battles in the history of the U.S. Marine Corps.

Rikihei Inoguchi, Tadashi Nakajima, and Roger Pineau, *The Divine Wind: Japan's Kamikaze Force in World War II.* New York: Ballantine Books, 1972. Two former Japanese naval officers relive the tragic ten-month history of Japan's unique suicide force.

Rikihei Inoguchi and Tadashi Nakajima, "The Kamikaze Attack Corps," *U.S. Naval Institute Proceedings.* Translated and condensed by Masataka Chihaya and Roger Pineau. September 1953, pp. 932–45. A short version of the authors' full-length book on the kamikazes.

Edward Jablonski, *Airwar,* vol. II. Garden City, NY: Doubleday, 1971. An illustrated history of aerial warfare during World War II, including an in-depth examination of the kamikaze phenomenon.

Yasuo Kuwahara and Gordon T. Allred, *Kamikaze.* New York: Ballantine Books, 1974. A Japanese pilot's own story of the suicide squadrons.

Raymond Lamont-Brown, *Kamikaze: Japan's Suicide Samurai.* London: Arms and Armour Press, 1997. Examines the kamikaze flights of World War II, not as a futile gesture but as Japan's determined last response to a war that was turning against her.

Robert Leckie, *Okinawa: The Last Battle of World War II*. New York: Viking, 1995. The U.S. Army, Navy, and Marines attack the Japanese-held island with 540,000 men and 1,600 ships; excellent coverage of the renowned kamikaze attacks.

Peter Maas, "The Battle of the Philippine Sea," in *Reader's Digest Illustrated Story of World War II*. Pleasantville, NY: Reader's Digest Association, 1969. An exciting account of the "Great Marianas Turkey Shoot."

Frank A. Manson, "Seventy-Nine Minutes on the Picket Line," *U.S. Naval Institute Proceedings, September* 1949, pp. 996–1,003. A naval commander describes one of the toughest single destroyer-kamikaze battles of the Second World War.

Henri Michel, *The Second World War*, vol. 2. Translated by Douglas Parmée. New York: Praeger, 1975. Contains selective coverage of the Allies' conquest of Japan in Asia and the Pacific.

Nathan Miller, *War at Sea: A Naval History of World War II*. New York: Scribner, 1995. A comprehensive history of sea warfare for the general reader that details the operations of all the combatants.

Bernard Millot, *Divine Thunder: The Life and Death of the Kamikazes*. New York: Pinnacle Books, 1970. A riveting account of Japan's suicide pilots and their devastating assaults against Allied forces in World War II.

Ryuji Nagatsuka, *I Was a Kamikaze*. Translated by Nina Rootes. New York: Macmillan, 1972. A surviving kamikaze tells what motivated Japan's suicide pilots and what it was like to face almost certain death on a mission.

Hatsuho Naito, *Thunder Gods: The Kamikaze Pilots Tell Their Story*. New York: Kodansha International, 1989. A compelling first-hand account of the pilots who pledged themselves to die for their emperor in the closing days of the Pacific War.

Masatake Okumiya and Jiro Horikoshi, with Martin Caidin, *Zero!* New York: Ballantine Books, 1973. The story of Japan's air war in the Pacific, 1941–1945.

Roger Pineau, "Spirit of the Divine Wind," *U.S. Naval Institute Proceedings*, November 1958, pp. 22–29. The author probes the core of the kamikaze attitude toward duty and suicide missions.

Clark G. Reynolds and the Editors of Time-Life Books, *The Carrier War*. The Epic of Flight series. Alexandria, VA: Time-Life Books, 1982. An impressively written and illustrated history of carrier warfare during the Second World War.

Saburo Sakai, with Martin Caidin and Fred Saito, *Samurai!* New York: Ballantine Books, 1972. The story of Japan's war in the air, told by her greatest surviving fighter ace of World War II.

Ronald H. Spector, *Eagle Against the Sun: The American War with Japan*. New York: The

Free Press, 1985. A broad history and compelling reassessment of U.S. and Japanese strategies during World War II offering some provocative interpretations.

Russell Spurr, *A Glorious Way to Die: The Kamikaze Mission of the Battleship* Yamato, *April 1945*. New York: Newmarket Press, 1981. Spurr re-creates the final days of Japan's greatest battleship as she sails to her doom during the death knell of the Imperial Japanese Navy.

Jack Stenbuck, ed., *Typewriter Battalion: Dramatic Frontline Dispatches from World War II*. New York: William Morrow, 1995. Actual words from war correspondents who reported day to day, battle by battle, from the war front in World War II.

C. L. Sulzberger, *World War II*. New York: American Heritage Press, 1985. A superb treatise on the war years, written in an engrossing style for the lay reader.

Yuri Tanaka, *Hidden Horrors: Japanese War Crimes in World War II*. New York: Westview Press, 1996. Tanaka documents for the first time previously hidden Japanese atrocities in World War II.

John Toland, *The Rising Sun: The Decline and Fall of the Japanese Empire, 1936–1945*, 2 vols. New York: Random House, 1970. A narrative history of Japan from the invasion of Manchuria to the atom bomb.

Stephen Turnbull, *Samurai: The Warrior Tradition*. London: Arms and Armour Press, 1996. An authoritative coverage of the costume, equipment, and character of the Japanese samurai.

Bertram Vogel, "Who Were the *Kamikaze*?" *U.S. Naval Institute Proceedings*, July 1947, pp. 833–37. Vogel describes the military and psychological factors involved in the development of Japan's suicide attack corps.

Denis Warner and Peggy Warner, with Sadao Seno, *The Sacred Warriors: Japan's Suicide Legions*. New York: Van Nostrand Reinhold Company, 1982. An intriguing story of the death throes of a proud and desperate nation.

R. L. Wehrmeister, "Divine Wind Over Okinawa," *U.S. Naval Institute Proceedings*, June 1957, pp. 632–41. A naval lieutenant details kamikaze action off Okinawa in the spring of 1945.

Tsunetomo Yamamoto, *Hagakure: The Book of the Samurai*. Translated by William Scott Wilson. New York: Avon Books, 1979. The story of an eighteenth-century samurai, told in his own words.

Toshiyuki Yokoi, with Roger Pineau, "Kamikazes and the Okinawa Campaign," *U.S. Naval Institute Proceedings*, May 1954, pp. 504–13. The author, chief of staff to the Japanese Fifth Air Fleet during the Okinawa campaign, describes kamikaze action from the Japanese perspective.

☆ Index ☆

★ Picture Credits ★

Cover photo: Corbis/Hulton-Deutsch Collection
AP/Wide World Photos, 99, 106
Archive Photos, 7, 11, 12, 19 (top), 23, 28
Courtesy Museum of Fine Arts, Boston, 17, 18
Corbis, 9, 10, 15, 38, 40 (bottom), 49, 50, 56, 58, 72 (bottom),
    73, 75, 80, 81, 84, 85, 88, 92
Corbis-Bettmann, 19 (bottom), 27, 29, 30, 35, 51, 57, 62, 65,
    66, 91 (top), 94, 98 (bottom), 104
Corbis/Hulton-Deutsch Collection, 5, 63, 83, 89
Corbis/Michael S. Yamashita, 22
Corbis/Museum of Flight, 67 (both)
Digital Stock, 32 (top), 34, 42, 55, 72 (top), 74, 78, 98 (top)
Lineworks, Incorporated, 31, 41
National Archives, 26, 32 (bottom), 33, 43
National Archives/Corbis, 52, 60, 101 (top), 102
Reuters/Kimimasa Mayama/Archive Photos, 20
Smithsonian Institution, 54, 59 (top), 70, 87, 101 (bottom)
Steichen Combat Prints/United States Naval Academy, 68
Stock Montage, Inc., 13, 24
UPI/Corbis-Bettmann, 37, 40 (top), 45, 59 (bottom), 95
U.S. Army Photograph, 91 (bottom)
Ward; Baldwin/Corbis-Bettmann, 77

✮ About the Author ✮

Earle Rice Jr. attended San Jose City College and Foothill College on the San Francisco peninsula, after serving nine years with the U.S. Marine Corps.

He has authored more than thirty books for young adults, including fast-action fiction and adaptations of *Dracula, All Quiet on the Western Front,* and *The Grapes of Wrath.* Mr. Rice has written seventeen books for Lucent, including *The Cuban Revolution, The Salem Witch Trials, The Final Solution, Nazi War Criminals, Life in the Middle Ages,* and seven books in the popular Great Battles series. He has also written articles, short stories, and miscellaneous website materials, and has previously worked for several years as a technical writer.

Mr. Rice is a former senior design engineer in the aerospace industry who now devotes full-time to his writing. He lives in Julian, California, with his wife, daughter, two granddaughters, four cats, and a dog.